Thinker
Nietzsche's Materialism

$12.95

Theory and History of Literature
Edited by Wlad Godzich and Jochen Schulte-Sasse

For other books in the series, see p. 107

Thinker on Stage:
Nietzsche's Materialism

Peter Sloterdijk

Translation by Jamie Owen Daniel

Foreword by Jochen Schulte-Sasse

Theory and History of Literature, Volume 56

University of Minnesota Press, Minneapolis

Published by the University of Minnesota Press
2037 University Avenue Southeast, Minneapolis, MN 55414.
Published simultaneously in Canada
by Fitzhenry & Whiteside Limited, Markham.
Printed in the United States of America.

Library of Congress Cataloging-in-Publication Data

Sloterdijk, Peter, 1947–
    [Denker auf der Bühne. English]
    Thinker on stage : Nietzsche's materialism / Peter Sloterdijk; translation by Jamie Owen Daniel; foreword by Jochen Schulte-Sasse.
        p.   cm. — (Theory and history of literature ; v. 56)
    Translation of: Der Denker auf der Bühne.
    Bibliography: p.
    Includes index.
    ISBN 0-8166-1764-3
    ISBN 0-8166-1765-1 (pbk.)
    1. Nietzsche, Friedrich Wilhelm, 1844-1900.   I. Title.
II. Series.
B3317.S5813   1989
1983—dc20   89-31941
                                                                    CIP

For Dietmar Kamper
in affectionate solidarity

"By no means," said Zarathustra. *"You have made danger your vocation; there is nothing contemptible in that. Now you perish of your vocation: for that I will bury you with my own hands."*

Zarathustra's Prologue

Contents

Foreword: Nietzsche's Theoretical Resistance
Jochen Schulte-Sasse

I

At first glance, Sloterdijk's book merely offers a rereading of Nietzsche's *The Birth of Tragedy out of the Spirit of Music* (1871). However, since the author takes this text to be one of the basic, central texts of modernity, his reading quickly reaches a point where it goes beyond being solely a commentary on Nietzsche's early treatise. It offers a rereading and a rethinking of some basic features of modernity as *reflected* and *thought through in Nietzsche's text*. In particular, Nietzsche's all-too-often misunderstood terminological opposition "Dionysian" versus "Apollonian" art (which turns out *not* to be an opposition) proves to be an important facet in Sloterdijk's rethinking of modernity.

Not very far into his essay, Sloterdijk feels compelled to reiterate a question usually associated with Max Weber and, more recently, with Jürgen Habermas: "Has not the division of the labor of talent that characterizes our times led to the tendential opposition of the psychic attitudes that capacitate scientifically oriented knowledge to the expression of the self, while those that accommodate self-expression betray a propensity that is hostile to knowledge? Are not the cults of science and aesthetics the prototypical 'complementary idiots' of modernity?" (S 12).[1] The Weberian-Habermasian answers to these questions are well known. Essentially, both Weber and Habermas—confirming the factual existence of the divisions induced by the process of modernization—view these divisions as progress. They perceive the adversity of instrumental knowledge and aesthetic self-expression not as hostility but as the result of a functional differentiation of social practices that should be evaluated positively as long as each and every one of the functionally differentiated social practices does not overstep the boundaries of its range. Habermas accuses Nietzsche of doing precisely the latter, namely, of elaborating upon strategies of intervention that, if widely adopted, would lead to a breakdown of the balanced system of functionally differentiated realms in modern societies. According to Habermas, Nietzsche's valorization of the Dionysian over the Apollonian is an early, avant-la-lettre expression of the so-called postmodern project, which tries to rupture the delicate balance of the system of modernity. Within this system—whose organizational mode Weber and Habermas, as cultural politicians, set out to defend against the alleged opposition of intellectual subverters like Nietzsche—the Other of reason is deferred to a delimited and relatively autonomous aesthetic realm. To be more precise, the aesthetic as the Other of reason is made to eschew its radical otherness and turn itself into reason's supplement. Thus, when Habermas charges postmodernism with hypostatizing ''the aesthetic, as the gate to the Dionysian, as the Other of reason,''[2] he presupposes that the Dionysian, once integrated into the functional differentiation of modernity and delimited within its own subsystem, can be turned into a necessary complement of reason or rationality, thus stabilizing the overall structure of the system.

According to Habermas's affirmative perception of modernity, Nietzsche—as critic of modernity—amplifies the Romantic contamination of the theoretical and moral with the aesthetic. How is such a contamination conceivable, and what are the premises of such a critique? From the viewpoint of modernity and its accompanying conception of individuality, subjectivity has to be constituted as a contained, agonistic entity. Nietzsche's valorization of the ''Dionysian,'' however, is alleged to express and stress the opposite principle, that is, the dissolution of ego boundaries. At first glance, such a statement seems to be more than accurate. For instance, Nietzsche holds that as ''Dionysian emotions . . . grow in intensity everything subjective vanishes into complete self-forgetfulness'' (N 36). In the state of Dionysian ego transgression, the agonistic individuality of competitive subjects is suspended in favor of a ''destruction of the principium individuationis'' (N 40). From a perspective affirming the social and psychic structures of modernity, the danger inherent in the Dionysian principle is apparent in *any* valorization of the Dionysian, even if the latter is delimited within the realm of art. That is to say, even if Dionysian reality is institutionally sealed off—in aesthetic experience—by a gulf of forgetting from the world of theoretical comprehension and moral activity (i.e., from everyday life), Dionysian art allows entry into a world of ecstasy—at the price of a painful un-differentiation or dissolution (*Entgrenzung*) of the individual, of an internal and external melting into amorphous nature.[3] By giving up its complementary functional role as a ''pendant [*Gegeninstanz*] to reason, '' the Dionysian mode of aesthetic experience, according to Habermas, assists in the practical and effective ''self-unveiling of a decentered form of subjectivity freed from all the limits of cognition and purpose, from all the imperatives of usefulness and morality.''[4] Habermas articulates anxieties that are widespread in contemporary Western cultures; he shares them with neoliberals and conservatives alike, fearing a dissolution of the psychic armor and moral centeredness of Western individuality.

Contrary to popular belief, however, a simple valorization of the Dionysian over the Apollonian takes place nowhere in Nietzsche. As far as art is concerned, the Dionysian is always tamed or at least contained through the irrevocable necessity of representing itself. Representation, however, is always already Apollonian in nature. As Sloterdijk explains: ''The orgiastic musical element is never in danger of breaking through the Apollonian barriers, for the stage itself, the tragic space—as Nietzsche constructed it—is, in keeping with his overall plan, nothing other than a sort of Apollonian catch mechanism that ensures that no orgy will result from the orgiastic song of the chorus. The music of the singing he-goats is a Dionysian paroxysm set apart in Apollonian quotation marks . . . In truth, the polarity between Apollo and Dionysus is not a turbulent opposition that vacillates freely between the two extremes . . . The Apollonian Unified Subject makes certain, through the mechanism of the silently established axiom of balance, that the Dionysian Other never comes into play as *itself*, but only as the dialectical or symmetrical Other to the Unified Subject. An Apollonian principle governs the antagonism between the Apollonian and the Dionysian'' (S 24-25).

The modernist's view of Nietzsche's discussion of the Dionysian principle, marred as it is by anxieties of dissolution, overlooks the fact that Nietzsche set out to think a form of interventionist reflexivity or reflexive resistance that tries to attune itself to the fact that subjectivity is not constituted as a self-same entity in ''modernity.'' Nietzsche's thinking of the Dionysian has to be placed in the tradition that conceives of reflexive reason as a force able to resist the instrumentalization of reason and its influence on social interaction. However, Nietzsche does not—in the vein of the early Romantics, for instance—place the subject, as a unified epistemological center, opposite an object designed to be ''reflected, '' be the latter other subjects, society as a whole, or nature. Rather, he follows the traces of the process of modernization *within* subjectivity and discovers in the process that resistance, if at all possible, has to begin by reflecting the split subjectivity of modern individuals. The most essential aspect of his argument is his insistence on the dialectical relationship between what he calls the Apollonian and the Dionysian—the structurally generated, contradictory desire of individuals to both transgress and fortify their ego boundaries.

Paradoxically, the dialectical conception of this relationship leads Nietzsche to a much more cogent and conclusive understanding of the basic division of knowledge and self-expression in modernity than is possible within the framework of a sociology of modernity shaped by a fundamental acceptance of modernity's desired mode of social organization. The affirmative reading of that organization has never been able to grasp the constant deferment that occurs when modern individuals strive for a unified subjectivity—a deferment that generates a desire that can never be satisfied and that, in the form of permanent projections of fulfilled presence, ruptures the very structure posited as homogeneous in prevalent philosophies of modernity. Nietzsche, on the other hand, tries to foreground and reflect precisely this very conflict inscribed in modern subjectivity. He does so by hiding behind a reading of antiquity and by narrating a myth, that is, by turning the conflict into one "between two deities who interact with each other like impulse and constraint, passion and control, release and moderation, movement and contemplation, compulsion and vision, music and image, will and representation" (S 25). Social philosophies conceived in the Weberian-Habermasian tradition labor to repress this conflict by detemporalizing the desire underlying the conflict and by projecting or unfolding it spatially into different institutional realms. The repressed, however, returns in the form of psychic structures whose split constitution is barely and compulsively covered up by gestures of exclusion and identification. Furthermore, any affirmation of the project of modernity that is at the center of these philosophies must lead, if politically successful, to cognitive ossifications—or into "metaphysical comfort," as Nietzsche circumscribed the modern tendency to arrest desire in sentimental projections of unity: for him, every affirmative perception of modernity's desired mode of organization must end in a consoling romanticism; Romantics, according to Nietzsche, tend to end " 'comforted,' as it is written, in spite of all self-education for seriousness and terror, 'comforted metaphysically'—in sum . . . as *Christians*." (N 26)

The tendency of an art integrated into the system of modernity is to comfort and to compensate for a lack experienced in other realms of social interaction; this tendency led Nietzsche to believe that the thrust of his argument cannot be understood by one who feels compelled to view modern history as progress. In his *Preface to Richard Wagner*, with which he introduced his *Birth of Tragedy*, Nietzsche thus maintains that "readers will find it offensive that an aesthetic problem should be taken so seriously," since "they are unable to consider art more than a pleasant sideline, a readily dispensable tinkling of bells that accompanies the 'seriousness of life' " (N 31). Because of the structural appropriation of the aesthetic in modernity, Nietzsche attempts to rethink aesthetic culture as a culture of resistance. However, he never posits a *different* aesthetic culture; rather, he simply connects features of modernity's aesthetic culture with the split constitution of subjectivity he observed in a different reading of that culture. In his view, the aesthetic as the traditional medium in which subjectivity expresses itself, may serve, if conceived differently, as a medium in which subjects reflect their own structural makeup. He attempts to shortcircuit aesthetic culture with theory. The conception and institutionalization of autonomous art as comfort do not allow for a radical reflexivity. The conception of such a radical reflexivity, which, as I will argue in detail here, is at the center of Nietzsche's *Birth of Trag-edy*, had to position Nietzsche in the eyes of social modernists in the camp of modernity's enemies.

II

Nietzsche's (and Sloterdijk's) renewed effort to uncover the basic conflicts and tensions in modernity leads to a reassessment of the dialectic of enlightenment. Habermas has also recently dealt with this issue by staging a rereading of Hork-heimer and Adorno's *Dialectic of Enlightenment*. Here, he denies that the basic (dialectical)tension of rationality and myth characteristic of modernity is insur-mountable. His reinterpretation of the dialectic of enlightenment essentially con-tends that the functional differentiation of modernity defuses and deactivates such tensions to the benefit of society, thus changing their dialectical nature. Slo-terdijk, on the other hand, insists with Nietzsche that the dialectic of enlighten-ment may be repressed but never overcome; he tries to recuperate an all-too-often overlooked aspect of the project of enlightenment—the idea of an enlightenment that resists repression and stresses the necessity for a stage on which the drama of the conflict is portrayed and worked through. As stated earlier, the principle that governs the tension between the Apollonian and the Dionysian and that guaran-tees the primacy of the former is that of the necessity of representation or sym-bolization. What determines the nature of aesthetic representation in modernity most strongly is the fact that a mode of representation enlightened by the basic tension between the Dionysian and the Apollonian can no longer claim to be a mimetic one. A split subjectivity can even less be "imitated," (i.e., objectively portrayed for an individual) than "reality," since the relationship between sub-ject and artistic object can no longer be one of an encounter with beauty; rather, the artistic object serves as a mirror in whose image the subject reflects his or her own constitution—a constitution that by definition cannot be "had" in a unified image. The existence of the tension between the Dionysian and the Apollonian forces aesthetic representations to incorporate into their being a reflection upon their nonspatial and nontemporal relationship. "Thus, Apollo is the calculating subject who enters into a daring game with his own dissolution" (S 29). Since a reflection, in the medium of the aesthetic, on the nature of this contradictory re-lationship introduces the only possibility of initiating awareness of the strictures of the system, Nietzsche can contend, in Sloterdijk's words, that through the "el-evation into the symbolic, the world becomes more than it was. The substitution is superior to what it replaces; what has arisen from the original surpasses it" (S 30).

It should be obvious at this point that Sloterdijk reads Nietzsche as Lyotard reads Kant. The Dionysian and the sublime are both unrepresentable, at least not without being "contaminated"—essentially changed by representation. Lyotard's notion of the sublime, although never mentioned by Sloterdijk, seems to be an important point of reference in Sloterdijk's discourse. For both Lyotard, in his reading of Kant, and Sloterdijk, in his reading of Nietzsche, emphasize the impossibility of symbolically representing an ''other'' space that is located outside reality—a representation that would enable us, by making a thinking of ''otherness'' possible, to intervene in reality. As a result, both Lyotard and Sloterdijk are concerned with the possibility of resistance *after* it has been acknowledged once and for all that it is impossible to represent a utopia. The belief in the *possibility* of such representations moved, as one will recall, the Enlightenment to hope that individuals and society—with the help of such representations, and through rational debates and actions based on such debates—can be led to a better future. In this sense, enlightenment and its philosophies of history have become ''impossible'' for both authors. However, Nietzsche, as Sloterdijk reads him, insists that this is an impoverished notion of enlightenment that tends to deflate the concept of critique as well as that of reflection.

Sloterdijk's reading of Nietzsche is an uncustomary one. In order to assess the validity of this reading and to grasp the nature and importance of the aesthetic state of radical reflexivity that Sloterdijk sees expressed in Nietzsche's book, I will turn to Nietzsche's text for a while and add my own reading of Nietzsche as a critic of modernity. As I will try to show, Nietzsche is a surprisingly structuralistic reader of modernity, an aspect somewhat neglected in Sloterdijk's restating of Nietzsche's project.

III

I already indicated that Nietzsche's reading of modernity, taken as a practice of structuralistic analysis, hides itself behind two rhetorical devices: first, behind the figures of Dionysus, Apollo, and Socrates, thus disguising its analytic force as a mythical narrative, and, second, behind a (pseudoscholarly) reading of antiquity. At first glance, Socrates' attitude toward Dionysus seems designed to illustrate and narrate the relationship between the functionally differentiated realms of the moral, political, and technological, on the one hand, and the aesthetic, on the other. Seen as a one-dimensional tension between two structurally unfolded realms, the aesthetic and the theoretical complement each other. The longing for ego transgression is, thus, the product of a structural factor. ''The idyllic shepherd of modern man is merely a counterfeit of the sum of cultural illusions that are allegedly nature'' (N 62). Idyllic scenes address ''the abstract man, untutored by myth'' and burdened by ''abstract education; abstract morality; abstract law; the abstract state'' (N 135). They are an expression of the ''diversion-craven luxuriousness'' of modern individuals (N 114). Speaking about the opera, which he sees as *the* ''thoroughly modern variety of art,'' Nietzsche maintains that modern ''art . . . responds to a powerful need, but it is a nonaesthetic need: the yearning for the idyllic, the faith in the primordial existence of the artistic and good man" (N 115). In light of his appraisal of the opera as the paradigmatic genre of compensatory art, he calls the historical emergence of opera, seemingly contradicting his earlier reading of Socrates as the paradigmatic figure of theoretical culture, "the birth of the theoretical man" (N 116). Yet Nietzsche is never interested in following a chronology or telling a "history," since every story is necessarily entangled in a nondialectical notion of enlightenment. Both Socrates and the opera are mere figures in whose images he strives to understand a structure without falling into the trap of a linear diachronic and synchronic thinking. "The [theoretical] man incapable of art creates for himself a kind of art precisely because he is the inartistic man as such" (N 116), thus compensating the one-sidedness of his theoretical existence. Like opera, the features of compensatory art "do not by any means exhibit the elegiac sorrow of an eternal loss, but rather the cheerfulness of eternal rediscovery, the comfortable delight in an idyllic reality which one can at least always imagine as real" (N 118).

Nietzsche's attack on such art could be and has been understood as an attack on the sentimentality of kitsch—as opposed to genuine art. Yet such a reading would not do justice to Nietzsche's argument; on the contrary, it would completely remain within the framework of modern "theoretical" culture, thus allying and implicating itself with that culture. In such a culture, a fully domesticated and structurally integrated art "rises like a sweetishly seductive column of vapor from the depth of the Socratic world view" (N 118). When Nietzsche contends that such a perception of art lies "entirely outside of the aesthetic province," since it is being "stolen over from a half-moral sphere into the artistic domain" (N 118), he accurately refers to the aestheticization of morality that had been taking place since the early eighteenth century and that found its earliest expression in writers like Shaftesbury. In this tradition, "sympathy"—a concept that was from the first decade of the eighteenth century to the 1780s undoubtedly the most important aesthetic category—could serve as an aesthetic notion stripped of its Dionysian dimension; it could represent an aesthetic experience that, as sentimentalized and thus domesticated desire, does not disrupt the system of modernity. Moreover, it could link the aesthetic with a philosophy of history in which modernity dreamed its own sublation in a future state of primordial unity.

Surprisingly enough, Nietzsche introduces the Dionysian principle in a terminology and from a viewpoint that is not only compatible with the Enlightenment notion of a pleasurable experience of community; it seems at times even identical to it: "Under the charm of the Dionysian not only is the union between man and man reaffirmed, but nature which has become alienated, hostile, or subjugated, celebrates once more her reconciliation with her lost son, man. . . . Now the slave is a free man; now all the rigid, hostile barriers that necessity, caprice, or 'impudent convention' have fixed between man and man are broken. Now, with the gospel of universal harmony, each one feels himself not only united, reconciled, and fused with his neighbor, but as one with him" (N 37). Nietzsche, the most outspoken polemicist imaginable when it comes to the Enlightenment notion of morality, introduces the Dionysian here in a language reminiscent of the hymnic celebration of community with which Schiller ends his essay *The Theater as a Moral Institution*. These initial similarities can be stretched even further. For Nietzsche's description of the Dionysian is also compatible with the enlightened or modern perception of the aesthetic as compensatory. Nietzsche starts from the same observations as Addison, Rousseau, Lord Kames (Henry Home), and Schiller, among others.[5] Yet, Enlightenment philosophers tend to view the relationship between the Dionysian and the Apollonian as a linear relationship between intoxication and constraint, transgression and delimitation, even then when historicizing it, they turn it into a pseudodialectical relationship between present and future. They not only tend to identify the Dionysian with the moral and political (sympathy), but also with the natural sign, thus erasing a problematic most essential for Nietzsche: the necessary and insurmountable delimitation and splitting of the Dionysian in and through representation.

However, the similarities do not and could not last long. For Nietzsche, the indispensable polarity of the Dionysian and the Apollonian began to swing out of balance in modernity. The occasion that induced this development was the gradual unconditional dominance of the Apollonian, restricted to the realm of autonomous art, thus stifling a mode of reflection that was geared toward human culture as a whole. The Dionysian, only simmering in art from afar, is—through the rhetorical strategies of aesthetic ideology—ceaselessly repressed by the constant affirmation of a newly differentiated and separated aesthetic realm. For Nietzsche, human culture has, ever since Socrates, been marked by what can be called a Dionysus oblivion. Therefore, no matter to what extent the concept of the Dionysian is seen in the tradition of aesthetic ego transgressions since the Enlightenment, Nietzsche vehemently opposes the Enlightenment's aspirations to transform and project the "mysterious primordial unity" into a historicophilosophical state that can be anticipated by "enlightened" intellectuals. He brands the transformation of the Dionysian into a historicophilosophical projection as an unfounded, structurally motivated optimism, "which, having once penetrated tragedy must gradually overgrow its Dionysian regions and impel it necessarily to self-destruction—to the death-leap into the bourgeois drama" (N 91). Wherever Nietzsche polemicizes against the Enlightenment and its global moralism, he does so because it deflates the dialectical nature of the tension between the Dionysian and Apollonian as the two basic principles of life, thus striving to neutralize the only space from which resistance might emerge. "For with respect to art," Socrates, "that despotic logician" and incarnation of the "theoretical man" (i.e., of the modern alienated individual Schiller describes in his *Letters on the Aesthetic Education of Humankind*), feels "a gap, a void, half a reproach, a possibly neglected duty'' (N 92). This very Socrates is therefore forced, at the end of his life, to address a question that he had constantly repressed and to ask himself: ''Perhaps there is a realm of wisdom from which the logician is exiled? Perhaps art is even a necessary correlative of, and supplement for science?'' (N 93). In short, Nietzsche saw the structural integration of the aesthetic into the system of modernity as a compensatory realm surprisingly clearly. Insofar as he attempts to rescue the aesthetic from such an integration, Nietzsche's project coincides with the project of the historical avant-garde.[6]

Nietzsche blocks an ''enlightened'' reading of the Dionysian by radicalizing the opposition between aesthetic and daily experiences: ''For the rapture of the Dionysian state with its annihilation of the ordinary bounds and limits of existence contains, while it lasts, a lethargic element in which all personal experiences of the past become immersed. This chasm of oblivion separates the worlds of everyday reality and of Dionysian reality. But as soon as this everyday reality re-enters consciousness, it is experienced as such, with nausea: an ascetic, will-negating mood is the fruit of these states'' (N 59-60). The aesthetic introduces the possibility of transcending agonistic individualism; as such it is a precondition for the acceptance of otherness.

Unlike the avant-garde, Nietzsche employs myths in order to understand the necessity for myths; he narrates myths in order to illuminate the nonmythical par excellence: social structures. The myth of the destruction of tragedy represents the functional integration of art as compensatory. Nietzsche, of course, could never agree with such a reading of his analytic method since it necessarily turns the mythical into an analogical construct that ''imitates'' a structural ''reality'' outside itself, thus defusing the disruptive power of the mythical. For if ''our understanding is to content itself with the perception of . . . analogies'' between history and society, on the one hand, and myth, on the other, then ''we are reduced to a frame of mind which makes impossible any reception of the mythical; for the myth wants to be experienced vividly as a unique example of a universality and truth that gaze into the infinite'' (N 107). Reading myth, as I have done, as a means of explaining the structure of modernity ends, in Nietzsche's view, in being caught in the premises of a nondialectical enlightenment. A structuralistic description of modernity that claims to explain the structure as a whole is an impossibility for him. The gap between the ''theoretical'' and the ''tragic'' can neither be comprehended scientifically nor deactivated. Only if we do not attempt to explain this gap away can society, ''leavened to the very lowest strata by this kind of culture, gradually [begin] to tremble with wanton agitations and desires'' (N 111). However, Nietzsche's inclination to avoid a structuralistic understanding of his own reading of modernity is, as I will argue later, based on the premise that a redefined aesthetic has to be kept from being contaminated by a social structure that remains ''outside'' and by discourses implicated by that structure. The analysis itself has to be turned into an aesthetic phenomenon. This assumes,

I would like to suggest, a problematic distinction between discursive genres. If one reconceives the same project as a strategy that can be employed *within* a theoretical discourse, Nietzsche's reluctance to employ means other than myth might turn out to be an unfounded epistemological precaution.

Nietzsche's essay displays an acute understanding of both the indispensable function and problematic status of representation. Viewing the "impulse which calls art into being as the complement and consummation of existence . . . a transfiguring mirror" (N 43), he conceives of the sign as a necessary complement to existence, since only in the mirror of the sign can humans free themselves reflectively from strictures inscribed upon their existence. Nietzsche's conception of the mythical or aesthetic sign as mirror has to be read as a political gesture of resistance. The sign, necessarily confining that which it signifies, is per definition of an Apollonian nature. By stressing the Apollonian nature of representation, Nietzsche insists on the necessity of delimitation; he even insists on the necessity of agonistic interaction: "For Apollo wants to grant repose to individual beings precisely by drawing boundaries between them and by again and again calling these to mind as the most sacred laws of the world, with his demands for self-knowledge and measure" (N 72). Self-knowledge and measure, however, cannot be attained in the self-same fashion of mirrorless reflection. Nietzsche cloaks even his epistemological and methodological reflections on the problematic status of analytic rationality in a mythical narrative. Thus, he expresses the status of mythical figures, prerequisite to cognition, in the figure of Socrates, whose image serves as a mirror in which Nietzsche can unfold his methodological self-reflexivity. If the Greeks had wanted to erase the influence of Socrates, Nietzsche maintains, they should have exiled him. The living, but geographically removed, Socrates could not have served as a sign (or, from the hindsight of a culture of the spectacle one might contend: at least not before the advent of mass communication). However, the "dying Socrates," being turned into an image through his death, "became the new ideal, never seen before"; and Greek youths prostrated themselves "before this image" (N 89). "Hence the image of the dying Socrates, as the human being whom knowledge and reasons have liberated from the fear of death, is the emblem that, above the entrance gate of science, reminds all of its mission—namely, to make existence appear comprehensible and thus justified; and if reasons do not suffice, *myth* has to come to their aid in the end—myth which I have just called the necessary consequence, indeed the purpose, of science" (N 96). Nietzsche argues repeatedly for a two-fold necessity of myth. The image of the dying Socrates is a mythical representation that strengthens the realm of science. Only in the image of its mythical representation can science sustain itself as a delimited unit; myth is a prerequisite for delimitations. The mythical image as mirror is the principium individuationis. In addition to such an *internal* mythical supplement, scientific or theoretical thinking needs an *external* complement: the Dionysian tamed by its artistic representation.

Representation—and the Apollonian as a philosophical reflection in the guise of myth is simply a mythical circumscription of the unavoidability of representation—"tears us out of the Dionysian universality and lets us find delight in individuals . . . it presents images of life to us, and incites us to comprehend in thought the core of life they contain. With the immense impact of the image, the concept, the ethical teaching, and the sympathetic emotion, the Apollinian tears man from his orgiastic self-annihilation and blinds him to the universality of the Dionysian process, deluding him into the image that he is seeing a single image of the world" (N 128). Representation detains and obstructs that which it aims to express.

Art as representation is "the mirror image in which the Dionysian man contemplates himself" (N 63). Like the chorus in the Greek tragedy, the Dionysian longing of modern beings "ever anew discharges itself in an Apollinian world of images" (N 65). Aesthetic representation is "ethical" and as such, it "exacts measure"; and, "to be able to maintain" measure, "self-knowledge" is required (N 46). That is, self-knowledge can be obtained only through the critical reflection of one's own split constitution in the medium of the aesthetic. Remaining self-reflectively aware that a poem is merely a representation, a "*mirror* of semblance" only (N 50), protects against dissolution and complete "destruction of the principium individuationis." When one "conceives of all nature," oneself included, "as willing, as desiring, as eternal longing . . . by means of images," one "rests in the calm sea of Apollinian contemplation."

In opposition to Kant's notion of an aesthetic idea and to the classical, related notion of the aesthetic contemplation of internally always complex artistic structures, Nietzsche insists that aesthetic experience should be one in which we "see at the same time" that we "also [long] to transcend all seeing" (N 140). What he expects of the tragic artist is a feature of all nondomesticated art: "With the Apollinian art sphere he [the tragic artist] shares the complete pleasure in mere appearance and in seeing, yet at the same time he negates this pleasure and finds a still higher satisfaction in the destruction of the visible world of mere appearance" (N 140). In regard to the necessity of representation, Apollo is indeed "the ruler in the antithetical relationship with his Other" (S 25). However, Nietzsche aims at establishing an aesthetic culture that allows Apollonian control to be momentarily, yet elusively suspended. Such moments are supposedly able to transform the dispersion of the (modern) psyche into the productive gesture of reflexivity. In this sense, Sloterdijk's remark that "Nietzsche's dramatic thought is in the process of discovering that it is absolutely impossible for self-reflection and identity—in the sense of an experience of unity that could lead to contentment—to occur simultaneously"(S 32) is even more pertinent. When aesthetic experience is turned into a reflection of the structural interdependence of subject and society/history, it generates a capacity to resist. Radical reflexivity leads to a split aesthetic state.

Nietzsche's own project wants to adhere to the possibility that "at the most essential point this Apollinian illusion" can be "broken and annihilated" (N 130). By reflecting upon the double necessity of delimitation and transgression in the medium of tragedy, "the Apollinian delusion reveals itself as what it really is—the veiling during the performance of the tragedy of the real Dionysian effect." Through such a reflection we force "the Apollinian drama . . . into a sphere where it begins to speak with Dionysian wisdom and even denies itself and its Apollinian visibility" (130). Again, Nietzsche's dream turns out to be the dream of avant-garde art, namely, that art might be employed to sublate its representational nature and to open up a space of structural independence. In this sense Nietzsche's statement that "Dionysus speaks the language of Apollo; and Apollo finally, the language of Dionysus" is the poetic veiling of a culture-revolutionary dream.

IV

Nietzsche's thinking starts from the tension between a phallic armoring of subjectivity and a boundary-dissolving ego transgression. Again, this distinction can be located in the tradition of the Enlightenment, particularly in the tradition of the distinction between the sublime and the beautiful. In Burke's essay *A Philosophical Enquiry into the Origin of Our Ideas of the Sublime and Beautiful* from 1757, for instance, which presents the first major (and most influential) theory of the sublime in the eighteenth century, the "sublime" refers to an aesthetic experience based on an armored subjectivity, the "beautiful" to one implying ego transgression. Burke bases his distinction between the sublime and the beautiful on that between "self-preservation and society,"[7] in which "society" means community. Whereas the beautiful implies a pleasurable relaxation of boundaries, the sublime connotes a painful drawing of boundaries: "The passions which belong to self-preservation, turn on pain and danger; they are simply painful when their causes immediately affect us; they are delightful when we have an idea of pain and danger, without being actually in such circumstances." He sees the source of this painful delight in the "absolute and entire solitude, that is, the total and perpetual exclusion from all society," concluding that "whatever excites this delight" is called sublime: "The passions belonging to self-preservation are the strongest of all the passions."[8]

It is not by chance that Burke closely relates the human drive for "self-preservation" to the antisocial or agonistic behavior of (male) individuals; that is, he sees agonistic behavior as a necessary attribute of the competitive and isolated existence of males. The sublime is the mode of experience in which males can enjoy aesthetically the peculiarities of their existence: "Whatever is fitted in any sort to excite the ideas of pain, and danger, that is to say, whatever is in any sort terrible, or is conversant about terrible objects, or operates in a manner analogous to terror, is a source of the sublime; that is, it is productive of the strongest emotion which the mind is capable of feeling.''[9] Interestingly enough, Burke values the sublime more than the beautiful. To him, the aesthetic reconciliation of the male principle of competitiveness with community seems to be more important than any reconciliation concerning woman. On the background of such valuations, it follows almost logically that Burke at one point defines the sublime as a phallic representation of a fortified, agonistic male consciousness: ''Now whatever either on good or upon bad grounds tends to raise a man in his own opinion, produces a sort of swelling and triumph that is extremely grateful to the human mind; and this swelling is never more perceived, nor operates with more force, than when without danger we are conversant with terrible objects, the mind always claiming to itself some part of the dignity and importance of the things which it contemplates.''[10]

I mention Burke's notion of the sublime here because it can serve as an excellent background for Nietzsche's recanting of this tradition. Nietzsche set out to dislodge an aesthetic culture that is centered on male fortifications, even where it institutionalizes momentary forms of ego transgression. He tries to establish an aesthetic culture that undermines the fortification of subjectivity. In this sense he conceives of the ''rebirth of Dionysus . . . as the end of individuation'' (N 74). Quoting Schopenhauer, he revalues ''the tremendous terror which seizes man when he is suddenly dumfounded by the cognitive form of phenomena because the principle of sufficient reason, in some one of its manifestations, seems to suffer an exception.'' The terror of psychic fortifications should be corrected by ''the blissful ecstasy that wells from the innermost depth of man, indeed of nature, at [the] collapse of the principium individuationis'' (N 36).

However, the Dionysian does not realize itself as forgetful ecstasy, but does so in decentering reflections. That is to say, in reflecting upon our split subjectivity, we release energies that dislodge an identity-bound perception of our selves. It is this aspect of Nietzsche's thinking that understandably interests Sloterdijk most. If a ''decentering of the subject, which bids a respectful adieu to the fiction of autonomy,'' is the sole means ''to a legitimate constitution of subjectivity— beyond ego and will,'' then the enlightened subject can ''no longer constitute itself as it had wanted to in accordance with the rules of Apollonian illusionism as an autonomous source of meaning, ethos, logic, and truth—but, instead, as something medial, cybernetic, eccentric, and Dionysian, as a site of sensibility within the ruling cycles of forces, as a point of alertness for the modulation of impersonal antagonisms, as a process of self-healing for primordial pain, and an instance of the self-composition of primordial pleasure'' (S 82). An aesthetic culture conceived as the site of such a decentering of subjectivity is incompatible with the aesthetic culture of modernity, which functions as an imaginary projection of the fulfillment of our dreams, be they personal or historicophilosophical.

Nietzsche's and Sloterdijk's readings of modernity's aesthetic culture are relevant to a number of current debates in the United States. To name just one: they are closely connected to crucial readings of narrative culture suggested by critics like Hayden White. In arguing "that narrative in general, from the folktale to the novel, from the annals to the fully realized 'history' has to do with the topics of law, legality, legitimacy, or, more generally, *authority*," White, for instance, holds that the narrativizing of events has nothing to do with an understanding of "reality" but is determined by a human desire to achieve a masterful, dominating position vis-à-vis external events, which, in turn, will allow the cognizing subject to conceive of his or her own ego as a knowledgeable, closed-off identity. The constant attempts by human beings to arrest meaning in ideological discourses and, thus, to interpret the texts of the world as transparent meanings is here viewed as the result of our anxieties that we may lose our identities. Falling into the other extreme, humans tend to fortify themselves as centered identities that enter communicative interactions as contests. As in the Greek competition, the *agonia*, the participants in communicative struggles are necessarily interested in boosting their identities, not only by winning in their struggle against each other, but — and this is supposedly the unsublatable presupposition of the agonistic character of human communication — by winning in the struggle against the perpetually mobile structure of language as well. Both the figurativeness of language and the structural dispersal of subjectivity lead to a need to safeguard human identity from what might become a dangerous vertigo. The result of this need to protect human identity is a return to a one-sidedly rational methodology based on the epistemological premise of absolute knowledge, the primacy of consciousness, the self-evidence of binary opposition, the priority of identity, unity, and homogeneity over difference, alterity, and heterogeneity.

Such considerations are closely related to concerns that *any* "value attached to narrativity in the representation of real events arises out of a desire to have real events display the coherence, integrity, fullness, and closure of an image of life that is and can only be imaginary."[11] White suggests, in the words of the volume's editor, that "narrativity as such tends to support orthodox and politically conservative social conditions and that the revolt against narrativity in modern historiography and literature is a revolt against the authority of the social system."[12]

The issues raised by White are, in the face of neoconservative and fundamentalist attempts at reviving cultural politics that are more suited to the erection of strong superegos, indeed seminal. Totalizing narratives which have a closed ideological structure unfolding in a narrative action from an ideologically distinct starting point to an equally distinct goal are the equivalent of a centered subjectivity; they function within the system of modernity as lightning rods and points of identification for a desire to achieve a unified identity—a desire generated by a split subjectivity. The narrative of ideological closure that assumes the possibility of ''a point of view from which the whole can be comprehended, a position, therefore, that must be essentially detached from and outside of what it seeks to contemplate,''[13] is—to return to Nietzsche's terminology—the objectification of the ''Apollinian illusionism'' that the subject can be ''an autonomous source of meaning, ethos, logic, and truth.'' The fluctuation in aesthetic experience between Apollonian and Dionysian readings is far removed from a *cognition* or *knowledge* of an aesthetic object; it has nothing to do with the ''acquisition of information about an object so that our subjecthood is defined in the cognition of objects, be they things, ideas, or other human beings.''[14] The only way to suspend the defusing effect of the institutionalization of autonomous art as a means of compensation might lie in the radical reflexivity unfolded in Nietzsche's project.

According to Nietzsche, disarming humans of polemical identities should be modernity's most urgent project. It is here where Sloterdijk can connect his reading of Nietzsche's *Birth of Tragedy* as a fundamental text of modernity with his own project as developed in the *Critique of Cynical Reason*, where he maintains that in order to survive, we will have to disidentify ourselves from everything that arms itself. The price for surviving in tomorrow's society might have to be paid in a psychic currency—or not at all. We might have to give up the security of all local identifications such as jingoistic patriotism that we achieve only at the cost of repressing alterity. Whatever fortifies itself in order to remain what it *imagines* itself to be, might dig its own grave. In Nietzsche's view, disarmament can be realized only as an *aesthetic* project—at least if and when an aesthetic culture can be established that releases the radical potential of the dialectic between the Apollonian and Dionysian dimension of art.

Notes

1. Using the abbreviations N and S, I will quote Sloterdijk and Nietzsche in the text; the Nietzsche text according to Friedrich Nietzsche, *The Birth of Tragedy and the Case of Wagner*, Walter Kaufmann, trans. and comm. (New York: Vintage, 1967).

2. Jürgen Habermas, *Der philosophische Diskurs der Moderne* (Frankfurt: Suhrkamp, 1985), p. 120.

3. Cf. Jürgen Habermas, ''Der Eintritt in die Postmoderne,'' *Merkur*, 37 (1983), p. 759.

4. Habermas, ''Postmoderne,'' p. 760.

5. Cf. my essays ''The Prestige of the Artist under Conditions of Modernity,'' in *Cultural Critique* no. 12 (Spring 1989); ''Imagination and Modernity, Or the Taming of the Human Mind,'' in *Cultural Critique* no. 5 (Winter 1987); and ''Art and the Sacrificial Structure of Modernity,'' afterword to Jay Caplan, *Framed Narratives: The Genealogy of the Beholder in Diderot* (Minneapolis: University of Minnesota Press, 1985).

6. See Peter Bürger, *Theory of the Avant-Garde*, trans. Michael Shaw (Minneapolis: University of Minnesota Press, 1984).

7. Edmund Burke, *A Philosophical Enquiry into the Origin of Our Ideas of the Sublime and Beautiful*, ed. J. T. Boulton (Notre Dame and London: University of Notre Dame Press, 1958), p. 38.

8. Ibid., p. 51.

9. Ibid., p. 39.

10. Ibid., pp. 50-51.

11. Hayden White, "The Value of Narrativity in the Representation of Reality," *On Narrative*, ed. W. J. T. Mitchell, (Chicago and London: University of Chicago Press, 1981), p. 23.

12. Mitchell, "Foreword," ibid., p. viii.

13. Sam Weber, *Institution and Interpretation* (Minneapolis: University of Minnesota Press, 1987), p. 54.

14. Cf. Wlad Godzich, "After the Storyteller . . . ," foreword to Ross Chambers, *Story and Situation: Narrative Seduction and the Power of Fiction* (Minneapolis: University of Minnesota Press, 1984), p. xviii-xix.

Preface

What I am presenting here is more than anything else a reading of Friedrich Nietzsche's early book, *The Birth of Tragedy out of the Spirit of Music* — a minor *étude* of one of the most fundamental texts of modernity, an occasional study (*Gelegenheitsarbeit*) in the most literal sense in that it was written at the suggestion of Gottfried Honnefelder.

In addition, this text offers an attempt to think of the concept of enlightenment in conjunction with that of the drama as a liberal continuation of several Nietzschean suggestions. Through this modification of the concept of what constitutes enlightenment, there developed an excess of commentary on the primary text — an excess that made it seem appropriate for me to publish these reflections independently, rather than as a postscript to Nietzsche's book, as I had originally intended. I would still remind the reader of how worthwhile — indeed, how inspiring — a close reading of Nietzsche's book on tragedy can be.

If the dramatic structure of enlightenment is borne in mind — if, therefore, rational thought assimilates its own phenomenological characteristic into its reflections — the tiresome theoretical self-misunderstanding that characterizes modern philosophy will collapse. Only a consciousness that is informed by drama, I believe, can escape the complementary disfigurements of a theory that has been cut loose and a practice that is out of control, thereby forcing it always to speak of the bastards created by a dialectic between the two. In the drama of conscious existence, it is not theory and practice that encounter each other, but enigma and transparency, phenomenon and insight. If enlightenment does occur, it does so not through the establishment of a dictatorship of lucidity but as the dramatic self-illumination of existence.

The ramifications of these insights for the self-interpretation of philosophy are extraordinary. As soon as it has gained a dramatic awareness of itself, it will cease to provide the world with mere opinions. The universal concept of philosophical thought will burst forth as a process of processes within which a world of worlds is written, experienced, gained by force, endured, stipulated, effected, and thought. Thus, philosophy will not be that which an alleged enlightenment had wanted to make of it, a resonant process of thinking by following along behind an existence that has always already just slipped past us. Philosophy will perhaps again be worthy of its name when it signifies the cocreation of universal poetry and a passionate involvement in the adventure that is called knowledge.

Thinker on Stage:
Nietzsche's Materialism

Chapter 1
Centauric Literature

For this reason, a higher culture must give to man a double brain, as it were two brain-ventricles, one for the perceptions of science, the other for those of non-science.

Human, All-Too-Human

The classic texts are those that survive their interpretations. The more they are dissected, the more elusive they seem. The more persistently they are wooed by the intellect, the more icily they stare past their transcendental suitors. And the deeper the forces of hermeneutical interpretative illumination and philological reconstruction penetrate the fabric woven by the classical text, the more adamantly that text resists the impact of interpretation.

Is it enough to explain the preponderance of the classical texts over their interpretations by stating that the successors of genius are always incapable of keeping up with it, or that it is impossible for commentators to exhaust the essence of the original? Perhaps a hundred years ago, when the humanities were in their infancy, it was still possible to believe that the resistant nature of the great texts could be accounted for in this way. A naive hermeneutics of this type was at home during a period in which the classical authors hovered, like secular gods, above those who had been born after them, kept aloft in an aura of heroic inaccessibility by an ardently worshiping culture. Their works lent credibility to the claim that their interpreters, as the professional ministrants of the intellect, waved their incense burners over the classical texts so as to translate the eternal truths contained therein into pared-down formulas that could be understood from the limited perspective of their own times.

This is not the case today. The interpreter no longer approaches the classical texts like a believer going to mass; the philological sciences have long since grown tired of their cryptotheological service to pedantic literalism. It has become increasingly more difficult for interpreters to believe that they have a

3

mission of any sort, and to compile their commentary on the classical writers in the name of the eternal intellect. Instead of plunging to whatever solemn depths to find the true significance of tradition, they have increasingly withdrawn into a methodologically refined indifference toward all the usual pretensions of the intellect. A text is there, and we are here; we stand like cold-blooded barbarians before a classical find (*Fundsache*), indifferent to the core, perplexedly turning it over in our hands. Is it still good for anything? In any case, we can no longer presume an a priori belief in the vital significance of the eminent text. At the utmost, this significance is revealed only when an ambitious critical ego wants to make use of the material to improve itself, or when, because of a topical interest, a useful quotation is pulled at random from a historical source.

And yet the drama is just now beginning, for it is precisely whenever disillusionment has done its job, and the succeeding generation of the intelligentsia (whether it has grown more mature or more cynical, it is in any case more moderate and skeptical) has learned to live with what it has inherited, that what is of consequence in the great texts is revealed. Just when everyone has stopped believing in them, they begin to speak to us in a new voice. When they are no longer given credit for meaning anything, they begin to enrich us in the most surprising way. When we have decided that they have no significance for us, they unobtrusively begin to reach out toward us. And just when we think that we have finally turned our backs on them and rid ourselves of them once and for all, they begin, slowly but irresistibly, to trail along behind us—not like persecutors or meddling teachers, but like inconspicuous ancestors and tutelary spirits, with whose generosity and discretion we are no longer accustomed to reckoning. When we have decided to concern ourselves henceforth only with our own particular problems and are ready to indulge in existential reductionism and shake off the all-too-excessive burden of it all, it is then that we discover the voices of the classical authors in the midst of what remains—an indispensable phrase here, a beautiful passage there, occasionally the stirrings of a kindred spirit. Scattered everywhere, these are the fragments of a vocabulary (*Wortschatz*) that we find ourselves unable to relinquish precisely when we have decided to deal only with our own affairs and to withdraw from the din of the media, the institutions, and the barrage of estranged information with which they bombard us.

Thus we are able to arrive at Nietzsche today. He should be read within this context—we must reckon with his new presence and acknowledge it as that of an author who is being allowed to return because he has been dismissed, and as that of a thinker upon whom we have stumbled because the subjects he deals with (even after the "clean-up") are themselves still present—annoying, brilliant, stimulating, and theatrical—and in every respect as unresolved as our own. And in doing so we need not pay the least attention to the official status of his thought and to the dubiousness of his ranking as a classical writer. It is too late to be racking our brains over whether Nietzsche, of all people, should have been elevated to the status of a classical writer, and whether he, as a man and a thinker, was the right choice to have been carried on the shoulders of an army of interpreters into the pantheon of thought. The history of reception does not, for the most part, trouble itself with the varying degrees of historical and human greatness, and thus Nietzsche has become a classical author because of a strange mixture of admiration and inaccuracy—even though, in his case, this has long since ceased to be the well-balanced classicism of bourgeois high culture, but is, instead, the wild classicism of the modern period, with its dark criticisms and its burning *dysangelia*.

Nevertheless, it has become common practice when discussing Nietzsche to remark that there are thinkers whose works can be studied independently of their biographies, and those whose life history and the development of their thought form an impenetrable unity. Nietzsche is said to belong to this latter category. We perceive in this platitudinous concept a trace of the injustice that can be done an author by comparing him to the classical authors. Nietzsche has not been mystified to quite that extent—his greatness has nothing to do with his being dead. Even if we disregard for the moment the almost inhuman brilliance of his later prose, Nietzsche's contemporary and mutilated aura has nothing in common with the irritating tone and noble boredom that are otherwise so often part of the classical climate.

But what is it that makes Nietzsche so contemporary now—indeed, so contemporary that even the admonitions that were raised against his teachings are once again notorious? What has made him once again questionable, quotable, and exemplary? Is it simply that our latest neuroses are in search of a philosophical protector? Or could it be that, after decades of dealing with socialist-liberal and born-again moralism, our *Zeitgeist* is again clamoring for harder truths and an enchanting removal of restraints? Has our pervasive doubt in the possibility of progress brought us to the point of needing alternative explanations for the phenomena of the modern period—explanations that create a distance between us and the monsters of history and phantoms of socialization? None of these assumptions is completely incorrect. But they cannot explain why it is Nietzsche's name that always comes to mind whenever we attempt to come to terms with the deepest self-doubt of the modern period and to make intellectual sense of the most difficult ambiguities of the present.

Before we delve deeper into one of the great texts of this author, I would like to suggest a hypothesis on the nature of Nietzsche's writing. Accordingly, his new presence could be explained not so much through his (undeniable) cultural-critical, psychological, and philosophical competence, the illuminative power of which is still apparent, but through a weakness that touches us more irresistibly than any strength. If Nietzsche is, as it were, still among us, it is less because of the advantages he has over us today than because of the inabilities he has in common with us. Nietzsche's most prophetic characteristic was his inability to be a specialist in any one discipline. He never allowed himself to be content with doing anything in a manner that was merely professionally correct; he never managed simply to do what was expected of him. Not that he would have been unable to meet the standards of any of the disciplines he pursued—the opposite was the case. Nietzsche's misery began and ended in the fact that he could never be satisfied with pursuing one and only one subject in accordance with the established rules of the art. Certainly, he *did* do this to an extent in that he was undoubtedly an exceptional philologist, an astute critic of his own times, and a profound analyst of morals, among other things. But whenever he pursued any one of these disciplines "correctly" (indeed, he was more than correct), he always practiced at least one other at the same time—and because of this was suspected of a general incorrectness. It may therefore appear at first glance as if, in his public life, Nietzsche had fallen victim to his own double gifts. His almost inexplicable lack of success during his own lifetime may have resulted from this (a lack of success for which his helpless capriciousness in dealing with his publishers is an insufficient explanation), as may have the explosive posthumous effect of his work. While any one of his talents, taken on its own and developed to a professional level, would have been sufficient for a respectable career—Nietzsche's career as a philologist indicated this—the combination of talents this man possessed caused him to lead the life of an obscure outsider on the fringes of organized cultural life. To speak of a combination here is incorrect, since Nietzsche's was not a case of the familiar phenomenon of multiple talents. In truth, Nietzsche's talents were not a collection of abilities that developed side by side; his talents were not really separate from one another, and did not simply coexist. It was much more that, in each instance, one talent functioned *through* another, so that he was not, like many artists, simultaneously an artist and a musician, a poet and a philosopher, a producer and a theoretician, and so on, but rather a musician as writer, a poet as philosopher, and a producer as theoretician. He did not practice the one discipline alongside the other, but practiced the one *by* practicing the other.

Nietzsche has taxed his audience with this plastic entwinement of his languages and talents up to the present; no one has played as wicked a game with the appearance of being easily comprehended as he has. Nietzsche can by no means be understood by relying simply on what is there in black and white and whatever else can be learned from a synopsis of the contents. Nietzsche's fascist readers were and remain those who prove to be massively boorish when dealing with the content, unable to comprehend his great game beyond semantics, his postmetaphysical music of gestures (*Gebärdenmusik*). The only reader who will ultimately be able to approach Nietzsche's undertaking will be the one who sees what this "many-stringed," displacéd, finely tuned author is really about when he puts something down on paper. Thomas Mann correctly noted that he who took Nietzsche literally—in the sense of remaining fixated on content and semantic reduction—was lost. Nietzsche himself was acutely aware of the indirect and mixed elements in his writing, and during his lifetime he was never willing to put aside the opinion that he was a composer who had been mistakenly driven to literature. He also sometimes thought of himself as a poor devil who had been driven away from humanity into the realm of acrobatic divinity—"only a fool, only a poet." During the period of his greatest self-confidence, he experienced himself as an expressive total phenomenon that was being evaluated only by philistines who used the usual literary, philological, and philosophical standards of measurement. He saw himself as a philosophizing counterpart to Richard Wagner, whose aesthetic demon was also not satisfied to express itself through a single genre, and who therefore came upon the idea of the *Gesamtkunstwerk*, a symbolic arrangement using multiple media and synesthesia through which he wanted to place himself totally in the limelight.

Nietzsche's originality is evident in the fact that he developed a literary staging process that had to make do without Wagner's operatic synesthesia. He had to trust his project entirely to writing, without this project being only literary in nature. Early on, friends and colleagues who were close to him realized that other forces were also at work within the psyche of the great stylist—musical and prophetic energies; Caesarian and religion-founding impulses; psychogogic, pedagogic, reformative and artistically demagogic drives. Nietzsche himself developed a minor theory of "displaced talents" vis-à-vis Wagner, and shrewdly noted that there was something of the actor in Wagner's natural disposition that, for lack of an appropriate stage for his outrageous pretensions, spilled over into the idea of creating his own universe in the music drama. But whereas Wagner, through constant self-expansion, transformed himself from rebellious composer into a composing cultural reformer, Nietzsche—"as a philologist and man of words"—had to compress the entire spectrum of his impulses into the narrow medium of writing.

Thus we arrive at Nietzsche's first work, *The Birth of Tragedy out of the Spirit of Music*. It is obligatory reading for anyone who seeks to maintain the ties between his life and the art of making sure that it will be impossible for him ever to become simply a scholar. This art, *nota bene,* is not a second-choice discipline for failed scholars, stolid philologists, or flabbergasted philosophers. On the contrary, the text is a matter of *philosophie et demi*, of a philology with wings, and of a scholarly discipline that had risen to the level of genuine philosophical reflection through objective/material intensity. As will be shown, *The Birth of Tragedy out of the Spirit of Music* represents at the same time the birth of the Gay Science out of the spirit of excess—even if this Gay Science might still appear here replete with all of Nietzsche's adolescent pleasure in being serious.

The phenomenon must be understood in context. In 1869, at the age of twenty-five and without having published anything previously, Nietzsche was offered the chair in classical philology at the University of Basel solely on the basis of the recommendation of his teacher (Friedrich Ritschl, the so-called pope of the Leipziger philologists) and thanks to a generously unbureaucratic gesture on the part of the authorities. In his letter of recommendation, Ritschl evaluated his candidate as follows:

> *Never yet* have I known a young man, or tried to help one along in my field as best I could, who was so mature as early and as young as this Nietzsche. . . . If—God grant—he lives long enough, I prophesy that he will one day stand in the front rank of German philology. . . . He is the idol and, without wishing it, the leader of the whole younger generation of philologists here in Leipzig, who . . . cannot wait to hear him as a lecturer. You will say, I describe a phenomenon. Well, that is just what he is—and at the same time pleasant and modest. Also a gifted musician, which is irrelevant here.[1]

Ritschl was mistaken on the last point—Nietzsche's musical nature had more to do with his existence as a philologist than his teacher was willing to admit in this moving and yet descriptive recommendation for the outsider without credentials. What Ritschl characterized as "irrelevant" within the context of the procedure for making the appointment proved immediately to be the one element essential to Nietzsche's existence in Basel. Ritschl had instinctively understood that Nietzsche was a "phenomenon," but he did not understand what was at the core of that phenomenon—Nietzsche's musical and theoretical double nature. By "musical," I do not mean only that he composed and played music in the narrower sense; rather, the whole troubled mass of what was grandiose and inexpressible at work within the young philologist must be included here, as must be the compulsiveness and urgent drive toward self-expression that made his life ambitious and overconfident—indeed, pregnant with ambition. Here we must also include the desire to be heard contained in his prophetic and reform-minded voices, behind which—without engaging in evasive diagnosis or obtrusive psychologizing—one can hear the voice of Karl Ludwig Nietzsche, the father he idealized, a Protestant minister who died young and whom he missed. Of course, the general elements in Nietzsche's case could be trivialized under the heading "The Rectory Releases Its Children," or, "If We Wake Up to Find That We Have Been Too Well-Trained."

In any case, music was already very much present in the first scholarly attempts of the newly appointed professor. His encounter with Wagner loosened the tongue of the scholar of letters; the musician began to perform through the instrument of philology. What this overgifted scholar had appropriated from Schopenhauer, Wagner, and the Greeks was this precise sensitivity to the modern resonances of antiquity, to the metaphysical content of music, and to the tragic greatness of the outsider. Here, in the first literary undertaking by the phenomenal scholar, all of these motifs sounded together for the first time in a great rhetorical orchestration. His centauric talent was in the process of discovering its own language—or, better put, its own languages.

Nietzsche's debut—a debut as brilliant as it was catastrophic—took place under these auspices in the winter of 1871–72. Its brilliance has become part of cultural history, as we are reminded in editions of his works. Its catastrophic element was to a great extent due to the fact that Nietzsche's vision of the birth of Greek tragedy contained more than the most well-meaning readers could have expected from it—even more than the author himself dared to realize at that stage in his development. The famous self-critical preface of 1886 sheds some light on the reason for this, and at the same time conceals it, because the later Nietzsche no longer wanted to acknowledge the superior—even though less ''manly''— elements in his earlier work. Its brilliance as a stylistic achievement notwithstanding, this ''Self-Criticism'' is a hypocritical one because, in it, the truth of the earlier Nietzsche—his insight into primordial pain (*Urschmerz*)—is stifled by the ''truth'' of his later work (the thesis on the will to power). This will remind us almost unavoidably of the analogous development in Freud, who sacrificed the truth of his earlier theory of seduction to the later ''truth'' of the theory of instinct.

Given the circumstances, a test of Nietzsche's talents was certainly appropriate. Nothing was more understandable than the author's need to prove that his appointment over better-qualified applicants not only reflected a fairy-tale privilege but was also objectively justified by the genuine superiority of the extraordinary scholar and thinker. What was called for, then, was self-representation, proof of his superiority, the corroboration of an academic rank that had been too easily won. He wanted more—he could do more. At his first opportunity to dazzle the general reading public, he immediately extended the oppressive excess of his vision beyond what was demanded by his subject.

That he did this is still baffling a hundred years after the fact. Who was really interested in the details of how Greek tragedy might have developed? Who, except for a few philologists of antiquity who were not interested in much else, would get excited about ancient he-goat choruses and the conjectured states of the souls of Attic theatergoers during Dionysian performances? Nietzsche must be credited for the fact that such obdurate lay questions no longer have to be seriously posed today. Because of his genial intervention, which intended in part to inspire philology and in part to force it to extend beyond itself, he made sure that the philosophical and psychological concerns of humanity could develop from out of the specialized concerns of philology—if one can use the term ''humanity'' within the context of current discourse without blushing.

It has often been remarked that Nietzsche's first book was, at bottom, simply a long conversation with Richard Wagner—a wooing of his fatherly friend and an ecstatic projection of himself into Wagner's heroic, immortalized dominion of art. Indeed, it is impossible to imagine *The Birth of Tragedy* without Wagner's influence—beginning with the ominous pairing of the gods Apollo and Dionysus, with whom Wagner had already been operating *pro domo*, and then continuing from the critique of the classical opera to the idea of a new German renaissance under the sign of a Wagnerian art of redemption. Nietzsche once made the coquettish observation that Wagner could have written the book better himself. And yet, understanding what influenced it does not grasp the phenomenon that came to fruition in *The Birth of Tragedy*. You can add together the Wagnerianism, the Schopenhauerian metaphysics, and the elements from classical philology any which way you will, and never come up with Nietzsche's result. For whatever the combination of sources and prototypes, the decisive element in it was the centauric birth, that is, the setting loose of an infinitely consequential artistic and philosophical double-natured eloquence within which Nietzsche's powers were bound together effectively for the first time. Only someone who has long since left his imagined audience behind him can write like this—someone who is no longer concerned with whether his actual audience will understand him. This would explain Nietzsche's somnambulistic self-assuredness in committing such a professional faux pas. In spite of his esoteric bravado, he was preaching to the heights, which were inhabited by his great kindred spirits, and woe to those who were not comfortable at those heights. "God have mercy on my philologists if they don't want to learn anything," wrote Nietzsche in the letter that accompanied the edition dedicated to Wagner in January of 1872.

It was to be expected that the word "megalomania" would sooner or later be used in reaction to such high-blown mannerisms—indeed, Ritschl was the first to use it. In contrast to this, Wagner reacted enthusiastically. According to Cosima Wagner, the maestro wept with joy when he read the young professor's book. This is not hard to believe if we remind ourselves that Wagner was merely reading the mirror image of his own thoughts in Nietzsche's words, and did not stop to consider that this kind of mirroring might also represent a provocation from a different sort of confident awareness of self. There can be no doubt that Nietzsche himself thought this and that he was attempting to understand his own development from the perspective of the dialectic of the divestment and finding of the self; in honoring the other man, he recognized an essential component in the process of liberating himself. Shortly after the publication of *The Birth of Tragedy*, Nietzsche expressed his obstinate opposition to total absorption in the cult of Wagner through an essay on the theory of competition in antiquity:

That is the core of the Hellenic notion of the contest: it abominates the rule of one and fears its dangers; it desires, as a *protection* against the genius, another genius. Every talent must unfold itself in fighting: that is the command of Hellenic popular pedagogy.[2]

This "cult of genius" (*Genialismus*), its curious and offensive aspects notwithstanding, will take on added significance with respect to psychology in our further deliberations. During Nietzsche's time, any engendering of centaurs was possible only within the context of a genial, artistic, "everything-is-permitted" climate, which later gave birth to these centaurs, these doubly destructive images from art and theory, stimulating fusions of the fundamental and the accidental. Even in 1870—after he had accepted the position at Basel and had, under the liberating influence of Wagner, made his first rhetorical attempts at a philology inspired by the spirit of reform—Nietzsche was able to express a presentiment of centauric literary tendencies. He wrote at this time to Erwin Rohde:

> Scholarship, art, and philosophy are growing together inside me to such an extent that one day I'm bound to give birth to centaurs.[3]

Only from behind the pretense of the cult of genius was Nietzsche able to defend himself publicly from his profession's demands that he limit his self-expression to topics that were customary within the profession, and that he deal privately with the so-called existential remainder. The genial mannerisms of the author can therefore be understood as indications of an understandable lack of willingness and as manifestations of an endearing incapacity—the unwillingness to mutilate himself academically, and the inability to be the sort of scholar who is interested in nothing outside of his own narrow specialization.

Now, it would seem as obvious as it would be misleading to understand Nietzsche's literary centaurs within the context of the essay form, and to thereby dismiss the drama of civilization that is hidden behind a reduction to genre definition by means of a prescribed phraseology, however generous it may be. The term "essay" itself has a cockeyed ring to it: it sounds almost like a plea for leniency in the face of insufficient intellectual powers. Its open form, its laxity in constructing an argument, the rhetorical liberties it takes, and the "vacation" it allows one from the task of having to provide evidence to support one's conclusions—all of this would point to mitigating circumstances. We are usually only able to associate such laxity with regression, and such liberties with a lapse. To the extent that the same types of tension-release mechanisms must coexist alongside a stringent intellect(ualism), the intellect that is dominated by professionalism and seriousness must concede the existence of a proviso that it calls "the essay"—wherein one does not have to be so particular.

But this is not at all true in Nietzsche's writing. When he lets himself go, the level of quality increases; when he opens the floodgates of his mind, the claims he makes are radicalized. And when he follows his whims, his discipline becomes more than it was. For this reason, Nietzsche's centaurs consistently take the wrong step—and thereby proceed upward!

The problem that begins to make itself apparent here is so extensive that it would seem justifiable to attempt to reformulate it. Might it not be true that, within the framework of an integrated existence (whatever that might be), knowledge of the world and self-expression belong close together—closer, in any case, than they are usually found to be under modern-day conditions? Has not the division of the labor of talent that characterizes our times led to the tendential opposition of the psychic attitudes that capacitate scientifically oriented knowledge to the expression of the self, while those that accommodate self-expression betray a propensity that is hostile to knowledge? Are not the cults of science and aesthetics the prototypical "complementary idiots" of modernity? And, under such conditions, must not the relationship between a cognitive modernity, as has been organized within the scope of science and technology, and an aesthetic modernity, as has been established within the arts today, be strained to the breaking point? Should we not instead perhaps simply speak of a relationship that is openly hostile?

If the situation is indeed as these questions imply, what are the ramifications for an individual who, contrary to the spirit of his times, still believes in the Goethean idea of a double intellect, which is simultaneously artistic and scientific? What happens to those naive, intense individuals who, from the start, have *not* understood that the modern promises of totality are nothing less than a swindle, pure and simple? How are those enthusiastic temperaments who are not quite up to the current standards for cynicism and intellectual dismemberment supposed to manage? With reference to the author of *The Birth of Tragedy,* I ask, Did the young Nietzsche drink his fill of Pfortenser humanism, the Schopenhauerian pathos of asceticism, and the Wagnerian cult of genius so that, in his own professional and journalistic endeavors, he could submit to the demands of the division of intellectual labor and allow himself to be restricted by the political tactics expected by his profession? "The whole man must move at once": Nietzsche could have chosen this adage from Addison, which Lichtenberg had once recorded approvingly in his notebook, as his own motto. Man must express himself as a whole self.

Perhaps Nietzsche's acute penetration into current intellectual sensibilities can be attributed to the fact that he reminds us of an unrelinquished dream of modernity: he succeeded, albeit at a high price, in being an artist *as* scholar-scientist and a scholar-scientist *as* artist. What we find so fascinating in this today is not the audacity of this solution but rather its obviousness. And yet, with his effortlessly effective double-natured observations as a scholarly-scientific aesthetician and an aesthetic scholar-scientist, he found himself caught in the position of representing an unclassifiable curiosity, which is at home nowhere because it could belong anywhere. From this eccentric position, Nietzsche called attention to what was a cultural and psychological scandal and an aberration of perceptions: the fact that what is obvious to any impartial intelligence is marveled at as representing something exceptional, and that what could not but spontaneously result from a healthy aversion to constriction was either celebrated or berated as exceeding a limit. In light of this, we can remove Nietzsche's obsession with genius from his successors without hesitation. What at one time could perhaps be accomplished only through the aristocratic pose of the cult of genius comes off today by way of an imperturbable lack of respect for limits. In the meantime, we no longer need even a superclever theory of deprofessionalization in order to resist scientogenous "specialists" and the nonintellectual spiritlessness of the division of intellectual labor. Resistance of this sort does not require any sort of expertise: of what use is Critical Theory if vigilance is enough?

But it *is* — in an outstanding way — a literary virtue. In order to be able to consider the current deficiencies in critical theories as a loss we can easily afford, we must perhaps simply cease to conceive of literature as a separate aesthetic world that, because of its specific characteristics (*Besonderheit*), has become a specialty in itself and, with this, merely a new pigeonhole. Perhaps literature is simply, in the broadest sense, the universal element within the centauric phenomenon. It would in that case be the *lingua franca* for free spirits, for those who cross the borders between spheres that shift away from each other, and for defenders of coherence. There have been sufficient indications for a long time now that this true. Always, whenever authors inspire a dual perspective through their own polylingualism, there comes into play the literary general eloquence of intelligent minds who seem to see the only value in limits as lying in the fact that these limits afford us the opportunity to exceed them. From E. T. A. Hoffmann to Sigmund Freud, from Søren Kierkegaard to Theodor W. Adorno, from Novalis to Robert Musil, from Heinrich Heine to Alexander Kluge, from Paul Valéry to Octavio Paz, from Bertolt Brecht to Michel Foucault, and from Walter Benjamin to Roland Barthes — in each instance, the most communicative minds have presented themselves as temperaments and variations of the centauric genius.

Whatever is at stake in *The Birth of Tragedy,* the appearance of this archetypal centauric writing took place within a conspicuous cultural vacuum and was met by an astonishing silence on the part of the public. According to them, the book was merely a private incident, a footnote to the Wagner cult. There were isolated readers who sensed that something promising was at work in this little book, but, in general, its immediate effect was to make its author appear to be "dead as far as his profession was concerned," in the words of Professor Usener of Bonn. But even those who sensed in this dense, moving opusculum the element that was rich in potential for the future would have been hard pressed to comment on what it was about. Only later, when *Zarathustra* had won Nietzsche worldwide stature, did what he intimated become clear. Nietzsche had constructed for himself a cultural stage upon which more than a Bayreuth renaissance was to be played out. It was a stage for exceptional disclosures, for cultural reevaluations of the most menacing sort, and for an unheard-of breakthrough into humanism by psychodynamics. The centauric philologist, who those around him expected would (devoted as he was to antiquity) carry on the cult of individuality of Weimar and Greece, raised the curtain on a stage upon which the bourgeois individual had to abandon himself to the most dangerous and at the same time most probable disillusionment. Suddenly, Greek antiquity was no longer a faithful mirror for humanistic self-stylization, nor a guarantee for reasonable moderation and proper bourgeois serenity. In one stroke, the autonomy of the classical subject was done away with. From above and from below, from the numinous and the animal realms, impersonal powers broke into the standardized form of the personality and turned it into a tumbling mat for dark and violent energies, an instrument of anonymous universal forces. Although, within the history of bourgeois culture, enthusiasm for Greece had consistently functioned as a key component in the makeup of the individual (with classical philology as the institutional support mechanism for the humanistic cult of personality), the most disquieting subversion of modern belief in the autonomy of the subject now arose from this, the most established of all disciplines.

Little wonder, then, that his colleagues anxiously restrained themselves. Only one man made the leap from embarrassment to outrage, restyling and transforming his unwillingness to understand into a condescending "I-know-better" attitude. This was Ulrich von Wilamowitz-Moellendorff, a doctoral candidate with the glib tongue of a professor who defended his academic inheritance before he had mastered it. Actually, he later made his career within the framework of the values he had attempted to protect from Nietzsche's subversion. The term "philology of the future," which Wilamowitz had coined to use against Nietzsche's book (a contemptuous reference to the Wagnerian "art of the future"), was a term of derision that became a prophecy—but not, to be sure, in the sense that Nietzsche's essay would point the way for the future study of classical languages and cultures. This term of mockery became true enough in the inversion of its meaning. Philological studies did not become more vital; rather, what was vital became more informed by philology. Through Nietzsche, a philology of the future was generated that, in an unprecedented manner, inquired into the correspondences between existence and language.

Chapter 2
The Philology of Existence, the Dramaturgy of Force

Is not hurt vanity the mother of all tragedies? . . . All the vain
are good actors: they act and they want people to enjoy looking
at them; all their spirit is behind this will. They enact
themselves; near them I love to look at life: that cures my
melancholy.

Thus Spoke Zarathustra,
"On Human Prudence"

It is characteristic of one type of important aesthetic theory that it never discusses
a phenomenon without incorporating some element of what is being discussed
into the discourse itself. *The Birth of Tragedy out of the Spirit of Music* is not only
a manifesto on the polarity between the Apollonian and Dionysian artistic drives,
but is itself the result of the interplay of energies that are both raging and resistant, intoxicating and precise. It does not concern itself merely with the occurrence of the Dionysian religion of art in antiquity, but instead directs itself toward
a verbal passion play based on old and new heroes with neoreligious gestures of
ecstasy. It not only addresses the origins of tragedy in universal human suffering
as it is manifested in music, but also presents itself as a rhetorical *notturno* within
which opinions that are too severe to be heard without producing despair can be
voiced from beneath a toned-down veil of well-formed sentences and attestations
of courage.

   Because it is a discourse on art that is nearly art itself, Nietzsche's early work
has become a model for much of what has been brought forth since then in the
field of aesthetic theory. It is a discourse in which subjects who have been trained
in science remind themselves of their extrascientific existence. Under the pretext
of a theory of antiquity, Nietzsche the philologist here devoted his attention to his
own existence and to the passions of the present. At the halfway point between
aesthetics and science, a new art of indirect confession arises.[1] For what, if not
the manifestation of his own psychodrama, can be at issue when an author extends himself (with a reckless sense of superiority) beyond historical facts in
order to outline a new image of Hellenic culture and its tragic psychospiritual

foundation—an image that exhibits traces of late romanticism and manifests a *fin de siècle* pathos, as though it were nothing more than a matter of translating Greek mythology into the metaphysics of bourgeois pessimism, and the suffering of the heroes of antiquity into modern-day gestures of inner discord? Within this context, however, the historical accuracy of the representation is less important than the intensity of the contemporary projection. On the path toward his inquiry into the self, the modern philologist stumbles upon traces of antiquity that can no longer be dealt with in philological terms. Similar to the way in which Schliemann exhumed the true dreams of his childhood from the ruins of hills that had been buried for millennia, Nietzsche brought to light, in the course of his philological excavations, a layer of tableaux that had been, so to speak, buried alive, the truth content of which was older and more acerbic than that of self-confident research into antiquity and modern-day manifestations of individualism. It is, in both cases, a matter of becoming valuable (*Fündigwerden*) in an almost psychoarchaeological sense. The singing he-goats who scream over the stage in Nietzsche's hallucinatory vision of antiquity are less ancient satyrs in a state of orgiastic ecstasy than exemplary modern subjects with their accursed good breeding and their cultural discontent.

Is it even possible here to persist in speaking of modern subjects? Is not the end result of Nietzsche's excavations into our cultural *archai* precisely the undermining of the new subject by the forces inherent in the old drama? Indeed, is it not, to a lesser extent, an undermining or subversion of the subject in a psychoanalytic sense, and much more an ontological derealizing (*Entwirklichung*), an inundation by impersonal energies, and the reduction of the subject to an effect of antagonistic forces and the conflicting "artistic instincts of nature"? The ego—and with it, its constitutive dream of autonomy—would thus represent merely the irreal seam at which the Dionysian force of vitality and sexuality encounters the Apollonian delight in vision and in dream. In the light of speculation of this kind, subjectivity (*Subjekthaftigkeit*) appears as the epiphenomenon within the interplay between the great subjectless cosmic forces, as an elusive interspace between the tendencies toward self-preservation and self-annihilation that exist within a cruelly exuberant and unintentional natural process.

The question arises as to what manner of philology this must be to acknowledge no fear when it questions the most sacred tenet of modernity, the moral dogma of the autonomy of the subject. When Nietzsche claims for himself the right to formulate a theory of the drama that then expands into a protohistory of subjectivity, he has ostentatiously placed himself upon a podium that no longer resembles his academic lectern and can no longer be considered a fundamental component of his role as a bourgeois academic.

But what kind of stage is it to which the philologist of the future ascends? Its cultural status was, in Nietzsche's time, anything but unequivocal, and has remained so to this day. This question cannot be answered even in terms of a quick association with depth psychology and psychoanalysis, because these are merely descriptively positive titles for something that radically defies clear definition, something that is evasive and negative. In any case, it would appear to be a stage upon which modern individuals act out a drama that (again, risking a falsely positive nomenclature) could be characterized as their search for self. Elevated to such a stage, theory becomes dramaturgically porous, and is permeated with the most powerfully instinctual existential tensions of those who do their thinking upon it. Thus even philology, initially so well behaved, can become adventurous. Within this context, theory is no longer a discursive mechanism that is served and reconstructed by the functionaries of thought, but instead represents a stage upon which life is transformed into an "experiment on the part of the perceiver."

He who steps out upon this stage wants to distinguish himself in a specific sense—his intention is to betray himself. But he wants to so do in order to force the dilemma, whose mask he feels himself to be, into plain view to the point at which it will betray itself. A mode of thought that has been existentially blown open in this way intends no affront toward so-called serious research, even if the latter—with its incurable dull-wittedness—understands it as such. Rather, its intention is to replenish the vital essence of this research. He who permits himself to think in this way does so not to get away with accomplishing less but to risk more. He who takes the stage as a thinker and takes a chance as a spokesman for an experimental existence must, from that point onward, assume an all-encompassing responsibility for the immediate and the indirect truth-value of his performance. At the same time, he has earned the right to have everything that he brings forward used against him "before the law"—against him, and, at the same time, in his defense—and this right means a great deal to anyone who has placed himself, by way of a radical self-sacrifice, beyond the shallow position of being simply either "for or against."

"Before the law"—this would indicate a second stage, upon which the adventurer of theory and the hero of thought no longer figures personally, but upon which, instead, his critics, his fans, and all those who, because of their openness to his suggestions, feel they have earned the right to hold the ground-breaking thinker accountable for his provocations. The extremely specific relationship between Nietzsche's writing and both his contemporary public and posterity can best be characterized through the image of the dual stage—one upon which the thinker exposes and implicates himself, and the other upon which those who agree with him and follow his thought test the applicability of the protagonist's truths to their own lives.

If a dramatized reflection is really an "experiment on the part of the perceiver," then the knowledge gained from this experimental arrangement must attract attention as the self-realizations of the thinker, while his mistakes are recognized as his personal failings. Thinking on stage is more likely to generate truth by following the archaic models of the wager or divine judgment than through the modern schematic of discursive inference from principles. In accordance with a totally apothecary concept of truth (*apothekarischen Wahrheitsbegriff*), what appears here as truth is not what has been proved to be theoretically the most logical, but rather what best proves itself within the context of a successful life. Whenever the thinker brings the truth about himself to light upon the stage, he reveals himself, *eo ipso,* in the process of becoming what he is. If he does not do so, he exposes the truth about himself and his hypothesis in that, like the heroes of antiquity, he succumbs to his dilemma and runs aground on his own inability to understand himself.

Whatever one thinks of Nietzsche, he must impress even his detractors in one respect, since, in his willingness to risk intellectual truths, he was the most audacious thinker of the new era. He paid the price for the danger inherent in his thinking to a degree unparalleled by almost anyone else. In his program for the stage, which was intended to lend him credibility as the new Dionysian hero, he ultimately proved himself to be above all else a hero of his own times, a hero of self-refutation. Posing and reflecting upon an open stage, he submitted himself to the laws of an unrelenting self-exposure. In his attempt to become what he was, he implicated himself in the most tortuous of comedies — so as to become what he was not: a hero, a superhuman, a "Superman" (*Übermann*). The greatest discovery made in his heroic search for truth was therefore an unintentional one: he brought to light the truth about heroism as representing the continuation of a fundamental violation.[2]

The first victim of Nietzsche's debut on the stage of truth was his standing within his own profession. One must first be familiar with what was common practice within the field of classical philology and its critical methodology, which, with its conjecturing and hairsplitting, was part renunciatory and part subordinate, before one can appreciate the grotesque gap between Nietzsche's attempt to push forward and what was customary within the field. What Nietzsche carried out was not a mere switch to a different specialization, a transfer from philology to philosophy; what he accomplished was nothing less than academic suicide. From this point forward, Nietzsche no longer addresses antiquity as a classical scholar. Whenever he does call upon the ancients, it is as a modern mystagogue and leader of orgies who always speaks from a perspective of inner simultaneity with the early Greek mysteries. Dionysus, Apollo, Ariadne, the Sphinx, the Minotaur, Silenus — from that point on, these are simply mythological names for contemporary forces and allegories for acute sensations of pain. Modernity is thus no longer merely a name given to a volcanic process of repulsion on the part of an undetermined present in the face of its own prehistory (*Vorzeit*); for Nietzsche, it becomes concurrently the almost accidental point of departure for the rediscovery of the basic truths of Greece. (As is the intellectual custom, Sigmund Freud proved himself a generation later to be the truest of Nietzsche's indirect students in that he also attempted to formulate his psychological opinions in the language of a time-obliterating modern mythology.)

But how is an "actualism" (*Aktualismus*) of this sort possible? How can a modern individual, contrary to all the rules of historical consciousness, want to place himself into a position of contemporaneousness with concepts that are so temporally and culturally far removed? What right does a modern thinker have to extinguish an interval of two thousand five hundred years so that he can talk about the drama of the ancient Greeks as though he were discussing an intimate personal experience? Two observations on Nietzsche's way of positioning himself on the stage of thought can provide us with answers to these questions.

First, even before he had voiced a single word upon the stage, Nietzsche was made ripe for it by his decision before the fact to present "something great" on the subject of the Greeks. What has been described here as his characteristic "cult of genius" refers not only to a psychic disposition on his part but also to a preliminary methodological decision on what his relationship with the historical material would be. As Faust called upon the spirit of the earth (*Erdgeist*), so Nietzsche calls upon the spirit of genius in early Greece to answer the question, How does one mind speak to another? And he himself provides the answer. The Greek world discusses its most puzzling mysteries to its greatest advantage with a certain professor in Basel who, because he is on scandalously intimate terms with Lady Antiquity, will one day be a former and ridiculed professor. Nietzsche's radical "actualism" is therefore an expression of his "cult of genius" vis-à-vis early Greek thought and poetry. The cult of genius, however, is to a substantial degree one of *concurrent* genius (*Kongenialismus*)—and consequently it results in the conviction that anything exceptional can be understood only by its equal; that is, greatness can be recognized only by an equal greatness, depth by an equal degree of depth, suffering by an equal suffering, and the heroic through an equal heroism. Nietzsche's concept of concurrent genius in any case forced the issue to such an extent that it conceived of the intellectual history of Europe as representing merely a spiritual migration on the part of the great intellects, whose path had led from Homer and Heraclitus to Kant and Schopenhauer and, through them, to Wagner and Nietzsche—a migration that always took place, of course, at the lonely heights where, aside from these thinkers, only eagles could survive.

The second prerequisite for Nietzsche's actualistic conjuring up of Hellenism lies in his historical-philosophical claims. Whenever Nietzsche takes the stage as a prophetic Greek scholar, he is wearing not only the mask of the genial hero of thought but also that of a philosopher of history or, more correctly, a mythologist of history. Equipped with its powers of authority, he condenses the past two thousand five hundred years—with a pathetic lack of concern—into a simple wave-like or circular movement. Accordingly, the initial depth of the early Greek tragic consciousness is lost in favor of a vulgar, optimistic conception of the world that succeeds in the form of a Socratic "enlightenment," the ruthless insipidity of which is eventually denounced and must lead sooner or later to the rebirth of a tragic consciousness. European intellectual history thus appears as the ebb and flow of a single motif that circles around or undulates between ascent, descent, and return. Nietzsche's construction of history possesses the primitive circularity of myth. What circles is a heroic pessimism that is born and dies like a living being, certain of being reborn. We observe here an archaic triad: the birth of tragedy out of the spirit of music, the death of tragedy because of the optimistic leveling program of a so-called enlightenment, and the rebirth of tragedy out of the spirit of German music — by which he meant the music of the present, which bore the mark of Richard Wagner.[3]

He who speaks in such mythic formulas has ceased to report as a historian on things that have actually existed. He has left the dust-gray archives and entered the arena or, to put it a better way, the maternity ward in which European culture is reborn as a tragic one. In this way, the mythologist of history is transformed into a midwife at the rebirth of phenomena that will burst forth today or, at the latest, tomorrow. Even this formulation does not go far enough: Nietzsche cannot be content to sit as a kind of tragic gynecologist before the birth canal of the intellect and wait for whatever might appear. He himself begins, surreptitiously and yet as if he were being enticed by an irresistible allure, to play the role of the one who is again giving birth. In the ardor of his prophecy, he simultaneously becomes the pregnant mother, the gynecologist, and the divine child. In representing himself as the assistant present at the rebirth, Nietzsche was no doubt alluding to Wagner, the musical orgy leader, who had once again lifted the musical drama of the present to tragic heights — but in making this allusion he also included himself as its fulfiller, incarnate *logos* and true son, in whom the master could be well pleased.

In doing this, Nietzsche drew attention not to the epic but rather to the dramatic basic structure of modern philosophies of history. For that which occurs on the level of greatness is staged not in terms of narrative but of in terms of theater.[4] However peaceful the tone might be in which one expresses these historical-philosophical theses, they always include the dramatic intervention of the speaker in a phenomenon that is understood as one of universal historical importance. He who proclaims a theory of progress inevitably includes himself as a participant, supporter, and culmination point in the drama of progress; he who presents a theory of decline asserts himself as someone affected by that decline, whether this takes the form of lamentation, resignation, or simply standing one's ground. He who diagnoses rebirths or periods of change brings himself into play as an obstetrician, an agent of change, or even as a candidate for reincarnation. And, finally, he who prophesies decline declares himself a *moribundus,* a practitioner of euthanasia, a hired mourner, or ultimately someone who exploits the carrion of a dying culture. This was true of Spengler, who was not content with simply diagnosing the decline of the West, but who also presented himself as an exemplary, fatally clever (*sterbensklug*) latter-day barbarian who kept a stoic, cynical watch during the death agony of European civilization.

Viewed in this light, historical-philosophical speech acts are the speech acts of a cultural orientation par excellence. The description of one's own historical position determines the quality of one's historical pose. Where, however, should these speech acts be performed if not on the dramatic stage of thought, upon which the engaged actors themselves intervene in the fate of their culture? We are able to recognize in Nietzsche more clearly than in anyone else—with Lenin being the only exception of equal stature—the fact that great historical-philosophical oratory allows the speaker to burst forth like a *force majeure*, whereby this oratory reaches a crisis point in a self-realization as a proclamation of self on the part of the speaker, and not without this realization being inserted most narrowly into the tendencies and potentiality of the moment. He who speaks like a modern mythologist of history always does so because the time for it is ripe within him. For this reason, the choice of words governed by convenience (*Gelegenheit*) also comprises consistently "kairological" (*kairologische*) phenomena, by which I mean, in the highest sense of the term, timely condensations of circumstances into phenomenological verbalizations and personifications. The thinker on the stage does not speak as a fool so much on his own initiative; rather, he speaks—in that he is pursuing his own concern—in the name of the "universal moment" that is being interpreted through him. The subjectivity of the speaker is elevated by this, purified of the interests of arrogance, and transformed into a phenomenon. Every essential historical moment is, however—as Walter Benjamin knew—a "moment of danger," and it is this danger that mediates all subjectivity. Thus, one can also say—presuming a slight taste for dark formulation—that it is not the thinker who is engaging himself and thinking. Rather, it is this danger that engages itself and thinks through him.

We must be adamant on this point: from behind the camouflage of genius and a historical-mythological enthusiasm, Nietzsche is able to set about discussing his concept of Hellenism with an unrestrained sense of contemporaneity. From here on, historical references serve only as a *foundation* for the performance of the most contemporary of plays. To be sure, the fable upon which Nietzsche bases his attempt is of an archetypal simplicity, as elementary as the most ancient philosophy and as monotonic as archaic music. What is a human being? What is the world? Why must the world cause us to suffer—and how can we be released from this suffering? These questions have an almost flat and superficial ring when measured against the shocking violence with which the isolated consciousness, awakened to the dilemma that is raging within it, is frightened by its own individuation and, after having been thus frightened, no longer *is* anything but the craving to understand what within it is really of any consequence. Who am I? What will be my fate? Why must I be "I"? There are no other questions.

In the initial stages of his performance, Nietzsche is still somewhat removed from reducing his undertaking to this primary form. This does not hinder him from already expressing himself within it—together with his Hellenist decorum, his Schopenhauerian vocabulary, his illusionist-rhetorical coquetry, and the educated-bourgeois cast of his drapery. None of this can alter the fact that in his first book (as will be the case in general in his later literary work), the dramatic primary structure of the search for the genuine self begins to function with great clarity. Motivated by a powerful need to express himself, the thinker steps out onto the stage, borne up by the certainty that his previous presentiments were sufficient to warrant making a spectacular entrance—whatever might still separate him from the latest views. Certainly, the actor does not yet know how his compulsion will express itself, and he is certain that the last word cannot be spoken for a long time yet. At the same time, because he is beset by the feeling that he is pregnant with great things, he is convinced that he has said something of the utmost significance—what else can a man do who is convinced that the greatest man of his time, Richard Wagner, has acknowledged him as an equal? The drama begins as if the actor wants to say, "I am here, but I am not yet myself. I must therefore become myself. I would therefore wager that what I really have to say will be revealed as the drama runs its course." This might possibly be the fundamental formulation of that thought that is marked by the dynamic between the search for self and the attempt to release oneself from it.[5] The thinker is not yet in possession of himself to such an extent that he can present himself to the world with the gesticulation of *Ecce Homo*, but he does promise that he will succeed in retrieving himself through a process of radical self-searching *coram publico*. The overall effect is as if his shadow should say to the wanderer, "If I pursue you with a sufficient degree of intensity, I will finally possess you." Or, the reverse, as if the wanderer were to say to the shadow, "I must first jump over you before I can arrive at myself."

As paradoxical as this all may sound, these duplications of the ego into the seeker and what is sought, the questioner and he who answers, the present self and the self that is yet to be, belong inexorably to the structure of an impassioned existential search for truth. (In Chapter 3 I will comment further on the paradoxical nature of the search as a means for avoiding the truth.)

In order to discover the truth about himself, therefore, the thinker must initially proceed from himself as relentlessly as he can because, otherwise, nothing else that could be found would be available for him—except for the nonobjective impulse. Like all of those who think creatively, Nietzsche must first rehearse what he has to say before he can know what he has been actually carrying within himself. This reminds us of the familiar joke: "How can I know what I am thinking before I have heard what I am saying." This makes it clear, in any case, that the joke has more descriptive power than the serious postulation that "thinking" precedes its expression. In truth, the joke illustrates in the most abbreviated form the structure of the search for truth. Therefore, he who seeks the truth about himself in a positive representation must first realize himself positively in order to find anything in this realization that would permit him to discover himself. For previously there had been, for lack of expression, nothing to discover because nothing had been expressed for lack of its having been sought.

Assuming that we are now in a position appropriately to follow Nietzsche's appearance as the announcer of another Hellenism, what does he say about the Greeks and, through them, about himself? To what extent could a new approach to the psychology of the Greek populace and Greek art also bring to light any truth about the reckless Greek scholar?

One can, I believe, summarize the fundamental assertions of Nietzsche's definition of the world as it is introduced to us in the book on tragedy in two statements. The first of these would be the following: the usual individual life is a hell made up of suffering, brutality, baseness, and entanglement, for which there is no more apt assessment than the dark wisdom of the Dionysian *Silenus* that the best thing for man would be to have never been born; the next best, to die as soon as possible. The second statement would read: this life is made bearable only by intoxication and by dreams, by this twofold path to ecstasy that is open to individuals for self-redemption. *The Birth of Tragedy* is to a great extent a paraphrase of this second statement and a fantasy on the possibility of unifying both forms of ecstasy in a single religious artistic phenomenon—a phenomenon Nietzsche identified as early Greek tragedy.

The path of intoxication is delegated to the god Dionysus and his orgiastic manifestations; the way of the dream to the god Apollo and his love for clarity, visibility, and beautiful limitation. To Dionysus belongs music and its narcotic and cathartic power; to Apollo belongs the epic *Mythos* with its blissful clarity and visionary effortlessness. The individual who is weighed down by everyday misery therefore has available to him these two paths for lifting himself out of his misery—two paths that can unite to form the royal path of a single tragic art, provided one has chosen one's birth date appropriately so that one can be incarnated either as an ancient Greek or a modern Wagnerian. Both paths, that of intoxication and that of the dream, concern themselves in different ways with the overcoming of individuation, which is the source of all suffering. Thus, intoxication has the power to lead the individual out of the limitations of his ego, in order to release him into the ocean of a cosmic unity of pain and pleasure, whereas the dream has the capacity to transfigure the individualized subjects as necessary forms of existence under the law of proportion, limitation, and beautiful form. The tragic work of art materializes when the Dionysian and Apollonian elements fuse with each other. This fusion takes place, for Nietzsche, under the Dionysian sign of intoxication because it comprehends the Apollonian elements of drama—the epic stage plot and the mythic fate of the hero—as only the dreams of the ecstatic chorus, which sees in the visible fates of the heroes objectifications of the suffering god Dionysus.

In fact, Nietzsche's book on tragedy is almost always fixed to the apparent dimension of its contents and read as a Dionysian manifesto. However, a dramaturgical reading leads with the greatest possible certainty to the opposite conclusion. What Nietzsche brings forth upon the stage is not so much the triumph of the Dionysian as its compulsion toward an Apollonian compromise. Even this reading would seem somewhat scandalous when compared to the classical image of Greek culture, because it no longer recognizes the serene authority of Apollo as self-evidently given, but instead teaches it as representing a courageous victory over an alternative world of dark and obscene forces. This does not alter the fact that in Nietzsche, from the dramaturgical perspective, the Apollonian world of illusion has the last word—whether or not this illusion dances henceforth before our eyes with an infinitely deeper opalescence. It is almost as if the humanistic enthusiasts of Greek culture were suddenly being expected to acknowledge that this beautiful Apollonian man's world actually represented a Dionysian transvestite theater and that, in the future, there could be no more relying on the edifying unequivocality of the Apollonian empire of light.

If one examined closely the fabric of Nietzsche's tragic universe, one would deliberately have to falsify one's gaze to not perceive that, in Nietzsche, the Dionysian element is never in power as such. The orgiastic musical element is never in danger of breaking through the Apollonian barriers, for the stage itself, the tragic space—as Nietzsche constructed it—is, in keeping with his overall plan, nothing other than a sort of Apollonian catch mechanism that ensures that no orgy will result from the orgiastic song of the chorus. The music of the singing he-goats is a Dionysian paroxysm set apart in Apollonian quotation marks. And only because the quotation marks are summoned in order to make the sounds of Dionysian savagery palatable for the stage are the great dark driving forces able, their impersonal casualness (*Unständigkeit*) notwithstanding, to bring forth their contribution to a higher culture. Within this arrangement, the impossible can also be raised to the surface—provided it acquiesces to the Apollonian quotation marks, that is, to the compulsion to articulate, symbolize, disembody, represent. Without these quotation marks there would be, so to speak, no performance rights granted. Only when the passions have promised to behave as they should are they permitted to conduct themselves as they wish. The price paid for the freedom of art is the constraint imposed upon it.

Nietzsche's appearance on stage thus assumes a profile that goes beyond empty pretensions. If we only saw it previously in its most superficial appearance on stage masked by the cult of genius and its mythological pathos, it now puts on a second mask, penetrating deeper into itself and into the ancient presentation of the play. From this moment on, the empty craving for and formless claim to a great self become a stage phenomenon of illuminating metaphoricalness. Nietzsche's second masking as a Greek scholar tells us that this self has borne itself into a conflict, and that this conflict is between two deities who interact with each other like impulse and constraint, passion and control, release and moderation, movement and contemplation, compulsion and vision, music and image, will and representation.

In our further discussion, we must accept that everything that happens on stage is being impelled forward by a conflict within the actor, a conflict that is intended to be reflected in the opposition between the two deities of art. It does seem, however, as if Nietzsche was unwilling actually to settle this conflict. To a much greater extent, he insisted on exposing it as something that was, to a certain degree, meant to stand before us as an eternal polarity, comparable to a sculpture carved in stone of two superhuman wrestlers whose potential for violence is immediately apparent to anyone without their ever having to move. Both deities seem to have been frozen in a vision of struggling movement.

What is the significance of this state of affairs? We must first understand what it was that Nietzsche was decreeing with such great determination. Apollo and Dionysus, after an initial tug-of-war, counterbalance each other and have our interests at heart exclusively in their compromise. A resulting attention to symmetry, to a principle of equilibrium (*Isosthenie*), can therefore be attributed to Nietzsche's second mask; however, the idea of a balance is nowhere established conscientiously as such, but is instead inserted in a manner that is as surreptitious as it is energetic. In truth, the polarity between Apollo and Dionysus is not a turbulent opposition that vacillates freely between the two extremes; we are dealing much more here with a stationary polarity that leads to a clandestine doubling of the Apollonian. The Apollonian Unified Subject (*Eine*) makes certain, through the mechanism of the silently established axiom of balance, that the Dionysian Other never comes into play as *itself*, but only as the dialectical or symmetrical Other to the Unified Subject. An Apollonian principle governs the antagonism between the Apollonian and the Dionysian. This permits us to understand why Nietzsche, although he presents himself as the herald of the Dionysian, at the same time perpetually appears with the demeanor of heroic self-control, to such an extent that what must control itself is named, emphasized, and celebrated as a Dionysian musical force—but always with the sort of emphasis whereby what is stressed remains under Apollonian control. Apollo is, even within Nietzsche himself, the ruler in the antithetical relationship with his Other.

With the establishment of this symmetrically frozen mask made up of the two halves of the faces of both deities, Nietzsche accomplished a stroke of genius vis-à-vis self-representation that has fascinated us to this day. For, far from reproaching him for not "really" giving full license to the Dionysian—as we would imagine the case to be after a century of liberalization and desublimation—we must wonder at the mythological device that enabled him to open up the passage to the Dionysian a crack wider. Manfred Frank has demonstrated most impressively in his book *Der kommende Gott* (The god to come) that this device was not without preconditions, but that the groundwork for it had been laid by the thought of early romanticism and Richard Wagner.[6]

Nietzsche's thought is established within this Dionysian fissure. However, he who begins thinking with the fissure of origin must be prepared to accept, as a logical consequence, the condition of having escaped as also being one of dissolution and separation. Having made this acceptance possible within a cultural context is the greatest profoundly depth-psychological accomplishment of romantic symbolism.[7] Nietzsche is able to risk putting on the double mask of Apollo and Dionysus because, since romanticism, the motif of a psychological fissure had become culturally acceptable. Even for those who were the most narcissistically sensitive and chaste, this high-cultural symbolism had in the meantime made a noncontemptible means of expression available for ambivalent psychological self-representation. Nietzsche made use of the romantic capability for looking back from the rationality of the day into the reason of the night in order to scout out, in his own way, the Dionysian energetics of the foundation of being. We cannot overlook the fact that this represents an extremely mediated and guarded form of playing with primordial forces.[8]

The recollection of Dionysus is precisely *not* a naturalistic *Propädeutik* of barbarism; rather, it is the attempt to sink the foundation of culture deeper into an era of barbaric menace. In any case, Nietzsche's Dionysian fissure proves to be the most promising form for maintaining a relationship to that which precedes a conscious awareness of self—an arrangement to which one continually returns whenever the question arises as to how the Dionysian truths contained within the foundation of pain and pleasure (*Schmerzlustgrund*) can be "integrated" into the forms of modern life without our having to succumb to the barbaric risks of madness and violence. My observations with respect to Nietzsche's acknowledgment of symmetry and his opting for the submission of the Dionysian to the compulsion toward the symbolic corroborate the thesis that few nineteenth-century books are quite as Apollonian as *The Birth of Tragedy*. The extent to which it can also be read as a Dionysian text will become apparent in Chapter 4—if we imagine the esoteric concept of the "Dionysian" as representing philosophical "thought."

Nevertheless, what has been said must seem astonishing when dealing with an author who considered himself to be the rediscoverer of Dionysus. We cannot delude ourselves about one thing: whenever Nietzsche referred in his later work to *The Birth of Tragedy*, as he did in the famous "Attempt at a Self-Criticism" and in the preface to *Ecce Homo*, he did so in spite of all his reservations about the "immature" features of his first book, and was consistently aware that this book would be immortal because of its new understanding of the Dionysian. His own Dionysian reading of *The Birth of Tragedy* can be explained above all through the fact that, for the later Nietzsche, the word "Dionysian" was the equivalent of "anti-Christian," "heathen," "immoral," "tragic" — adjectives that correspond overwhelmingly to the tendencies of the book on its semantic level. But this thematic prominence of the Dionysian cannot diminish the fact of the dramaturgical supremacy of the Apollonian.

I suggest that we take a closer look at Nietzsche's construction of the Dionysian. This degree of exactness is justifiable, not least of all because, in the book on tragedy, there is one point at which the mystery of Nietzsche's Greek scholar concept of the Dionysian is laid bare — so bare, in fact, that there is nothing left that would require interpretation. Nietzsche exposes his Dionysian alchemy, that is, his talent for changing a he-goat into a musician, at this one point more clearly than anywhere else. Let us slowly read through this most important first chapter once again.

What is happening here? Before our eyes, Nietzsche splits the Dionysian throng into two severely differentiated, almost oppositional choruses, which relate to each other like culture and nature or like civilization and barbarism. According to the author, a "monstrous gap" separates the Dionysians of Greece from those of the barbarians, a gap the highly cultured individual will never again bridge — indeed, will never even be able to *want* to bridge. This gap will take on immeasurable significance for the theory of tragedy. We can convince ourselves of this whenever we wait for the moment at which the fictive procession of the approaching god with its followers rolls toward us, only to be divided at the very second at which the winged (*beschwingt*) classical philologist is attempting to join it. The element that had fascinated the philologist in the distant and as yet undivided view of this chorus of Dionysian throngs is too evident to require an explanation. For, from a distance and presuming a grandiose disregard for details, the vulgar chorus is condensed into a humanistic dream image with an irresistible power to entice:

> Under the charm of the Dionysian not only is the union between man and man reaffirmed, but nature which has become alienated, hostile, or subjugated, celebrates once more her reconciliation with her lost son, man. . . . Now the slave is a free man; now all the rigid, hostile barriers that necessity, caprice, or "impudent convention" have fixed between man and man are broken. Now, with the gospel of universal harmony, each one feels himself not only united, reconciled, and fused with his neighbor, but as one with him, as if the veil of *maya* had been torn aside and were now merely fluttering in tatters before the mysterious primordial unity. In song and dance man expresses himself as a member of a higher community. (*BT*, p. 37)

This is what Nietzsche has written — even though the reader might not believe his own eyes. If the text were to continue in the vein in which it has begun, *The Birth of Tragedy* would be read today as *The Socialist Manifesto*, one that would not have to shrink from being compared with *The Communist Manifesto*. The work would be read as the program for an aesthetic socialism and as the Magna Carta of a cosmic *fraternité*; one would glean from this book precisely those characteristics that only vestigially shared in the image of the corresponding political organizations and ideologies. But the temptation Nietzsche feels to enter into history as the spokesman for a Dionysian socialism lasts only for a second—just as long as it takes for the throngs of the deity to storm past at the appropriate historical distance—and the reconciliation with man and nature is directly demanded of no one.

As soon as proximity provides for the dissolution of an idealistic inexactitude, all previous premises are reversed. Admittedly, to the same extent that the fusion with the whole appeared as pure impossibility, nothing stood in the way of a sacrifice to the unattainable. But if the raving chorus of sounds, bodies, and appetites comes closer, the abyss of primordial origin is opened up into that to which the individualized subject cannot want to revert for anything in the world. Images of horror immediately rise up—images of fatal constriction and death by suffocation in the cavern of eros. What appeared previously as a blessed disentanglement is now seen as a horrible dismemberment; that which longing purported to crave now causes it to recoil in horror with a definite sense of nausea in the face of its realization. The impulse toward unification suddenly changes over into a frenzy of disintegration, and the eros of the return to the womb of earth and community is transformed into a panic of dissolution and revulsion at the prospect of the socialist vulvocracy (*Vulvokratie*).

This is the decisive moment. The bacchanalian festival procession is now split apart, and while the Dionysian barbarians continue to revel in their group rut, a noble minority branches off that has placed itself under the command of the Greek will to culture. And thus, away with the barbaric Dionysians of the Orient! Away with the orgiastic sexuality of the cult of spring! Away with the compulsion toward physical contact among the people and other unappetizing subjects! Away with this leftist, Green Party, all-embracing crudeness! An Apollonian intervention is demanded here; a masculine, self-aware, individualistic principle should intervene, one that would confront with its purity and selectivity any sort of obscene confusion. Before the common Dionysians can become Greek and Nietzschean Dionysians, they must be filtered through a sort of preliminary purification process. This I will call, following Nietzsche's description of it, the process of "Doric precensorship."

Early Hellenism erected, so we are told, a masculine dam to protect itself against the Dionysian flood. It heroically resisted the "extravagant sexual licentiousness" that was characteristic of the Walpurgis Nights of the barbarian Dionysus. The Doric dam construction was responsible whenever the "horrible 'witches' brew' of sensuality and cruelty" became "ineffective." The Dionysian/feminine attempts at inundation recoil against the "majestically rejecting attitude of Apollo" (*BT*, pp. 39–40).

What is worth noting here is the radical revaluation of the Dionysian. Suddenly it no longer appears as a principle that is bent on reconciling the world, because of which all human existence would for the first time be able to achieve its true goal, but rather as a primitive force of cultural destruction, an uncouth demonic danger of uncontrollable release and dissolution:

> For me the Doric state and Doric art are explicable only as a permanent military encampment of the Apollonian, only [as] incessant resistance to the titanic-barbaric nature of the Dionysian. (*BT*, p. 47)

For Nietzsche, then, the Doric process of precensorship existed in the initial stages of the Dionysian; it served to break the flood of the Dionysian against the dam of the Apollonian. The phenomenon of an art of ecstasy that has been tamed into submission to advanced culture develops for the first time out of the binary energetic complex of dam and flood, restraint and intoxication. In the beginning was the compromise—the play of force and counterforce, which became inextricably interlaced with each other for the purpose of reciprocal ascent. Nietzsche represents this compromise graphically and does not neglect to mention that the authority who has succeeded in reaching the compromise is Apollo, and *not* his irresponsible opponent! Thus, Apollo is the calculating subject who enters into a daring game with his own dissolution. After this same Apollo had finally reluctantly acknowledged the imperative of the demands of Dionysus, he decided— according to Nietzsche—to disarm his violent opponent by means of a "reconciliation." Nietzsche goes so far as to note that this is "a seasonably effected reconciliation" (*BT*, p. 39).

The importance of this process can hardly be overestimated, for it signifies nothing less than the primal scene of civilization—the historical compromise of Western culture. Because of the Apollonian compromise, the old orgiastic power of nature is forced upward and is welded once and for all to the register of the symbolic as artistic energy. In making this observation, Nietzsche was aware that he was speaking not of an arbitrary episode within the context of the history of Greek art but of an event that would prove fateful for all higher civilizing processes. "This reconciliation," he says, "is the most important moment in the history of the Greek cult," and here we might add, the most important transition along the path from archaic to highly advanced forms of living. It is almost unnecessary to state that these more highly developed forms bring with them an increase in fragility, an ascent by the living being toward more improbable, more perilous forms that are, as if unavoidably, enveloped in a haze of perversion. Through the inhibiting and intensifying act of power that the Apollonian compromise represents, the naive orgies of early human beings are transformed into the sentimental festival performances of more recent times. They are no longer "reversions[s] of man to the tiger and the ape," but progress toward "festivals of world redemption and days of transfiguration."

Only now does Nietzsche's Dionysian undertaking again come into play. After Doric precensorship and Apollonian resistance have done their job and erected adequate defenses, the author's fascination for the Dionysian component is able to reenter, a component that has now become completely music, completely dance, completely mystical participation and beautiful suffering — in short, every higher form of stepping outside of oneself that the reverential traditional term "tragedy" sidesteps. Just as soon as a distance from the vulgar procession of the satyrs has been symbolically reestablished, the transfiguration of the Dionysian begins anew. Bracketed within aesthetic parentheses and dramaturgical quotation marks, the singing he-goats are no longer libertines who regress to bestiality. Rather, they have been rejuvenated into the media for effecting a fusion with the foundation of being and the subjects of a musical socialism. The magic is repeated within a secure framework that serves as protection against the risks involved in an actual enchantment. From this point on, everything appears in its "second edition" — Dionysian revelers in place of Dionysian revelers, unification in place of unification, orgies in place of orgies. This process of "standing in place of something" is, however, conceived of as a process of beneficial substitution, and not merely as a forfeiture of the original. Within the context of this gain, culture begins to affirm itself as "culture-instead-of-savagery," and this quality of standing in place of something becomes the key to the mystery of the civilizing phenomenon. The ramifications of this for theories of truth will soon become apparent — in the next two chapters I will discuss the dramaturgy of substitution and the metaphysics of illusion.

Henceforth, the old Dionysian forces are permitted to overflow with a new licentiousness — in place of licentiousness — into the riverbed of symbolization. No wonder, then, that the path to Greek tragedy is accompanied by the "greatest exaltation of all symbolic faculties," indeed, by a "collective release of all symbolic powers." Through this elevation into the symbolic, the world becomes more than it was. The substitution is superior to what it replaces; what has arisen from the original surpasses it. "The essence of nature is now to be expressed symbolically; we need a new world of symbols" (*BT*, p. 40). In short, the barbaric he-goat has advanced to the status of civilized goat, and, if he were to think back on his wild youth (although this would have to be delayed a priori), could say to himself as a poststructuralist, "A symbol has inserted itself between me and my intoxication, a language has preceded my ability to be present only as myself [*Präsenz-bei-mir*], a discourse has taught my ecstasy to speak. But isn't it worth lamenting the fact that lamentation itself has become — a discourse?"

The Apollonian subject(ivity), however, now notices for the first time, albeit too late, the dilemma in which it has implicated itself by agreeing to a compromise with the Dionysian. From here on out it can no longer conceive of itself *aus sich selbst.* Apollo has lost the illusion of his own autonomy; in his attempts to reestablish it to the extent that he can, he must sink ever deeper into the discernment of his own lack of a foundation (*Bodenlosigkeit*). After he has glanced into the Dionysian abyss beneath the forms, Apollo is no longer able to believe in his substantial rationality and his masculine self-control. His initial hope of being able to negotiate a compromise with the Dionysian in which he will be able to preserve himself unaltered is revealed as an illusion. Without fail, Apollo is swept into the undertow of the Dionysian dissolution of identity. It undermines for him the idea that the beautiful illusion of his own self, with its glistening abstraction and its abundance of rational light, might in truth represent only an objectification of the amorphously suffering god, Dionysus.[9]

What does this all mean for the actor on the stage with his mask of the two deities? To what extent does this illuminate for him the structure of his own subjectivity? What does it profit his experience of himself to appear on stage in this way? The thinking mime is, I believe, now able to recognize that he himself is not a ''One,'' a Unified Subject, but rather a dual subject who dreams of being able to possess himself as one. This dual existence no longer has the amorphous quality of an unformulated yearning and the pretentious pathos of he who feels that he is pregnant with his own self. This dual existence defines itself within the context of a thinking uneasiness — rigorous fluctuation in reflection between the Apollonian and Dionysian dimensions of the mask. This uneasily repeated fluctuation establishes the pattern of thought for an all-penetrating critical distrust. A mechanism transformed Nietzsche into a philosopher: the Apollonian in him suspected that he was at bottom only a Dionysian ''phenomenon,'' while the Dionysian saw through himself with the penetrating clairvoyancy of one who is reminded of his Apollonian castration. He feels like a mere civilized satyr, like a he-goat in place of a he-goat, who can no longer believe in himself because he must understand that his present self is only a substitute for his true self.

In this way, Nietzsche has set in motion an unprecedented intellectual psychodrama. Through his audacious game with the double mask of the deities, he has made of himself a genius of self-knowledge as self-accusation. He has become a psychologist spontaneously — he has become the first philosopher to be a psychologist as philosopher; his antiquating role playing has set him on this path. Nietzsche always finds himself in a position in which he faces himself as a transparent phenomenon: he does not believe in himself as Dionysus because he has had to sacrifice his wild lower half to the Apollonian compromise. Conversely, he has just as little belief in himself as Apollo because he suspects himself of being merely a veil before the Dionysian. The self of the thinker on stage that is in search of itself oscillates, within the confines of a sensational reflexivity, back and forth between the frozen halves of his mask. He relinquishes himself to a circular process of total self-distrust, which in time will mount into a distrust of all ''truths'' and all surrogates — but which at the same time rises up in a despairing praise of the illusion of autonomy and the divine impenetrability of the phenomenal. Whatever position the ego may assume, whatever "representation" of itself it may choose to offer, it will perpetually sense that the other side, the displaced aspect, is lacking.

Within the framework of this knowledge-laden, confused fluctuation between the processes of masking and unmasking, Nietzsche's third face develops, with dramaturgical repercussions of the most impressive kind. It is the mask of Nietzsche the "philosopher," the psychologist, the critic of knowledge, the thought dancer, the teacher of the affirmative pretense (*Verstellung*). With this third face, Nietzsche begins to come dangerously close to his "Become who you are" — dangerous because this mask, in its misleading optimism, could induce Narcissus to tumble into his own image. The danger that emanates from the image always strikes the person who passionately desires at his weakest point — the fact that he would like to have "in reality" what he allows himself to have only in the image, in the imaginary *modus* of representation. Dionysus does not permit himself to possess, and whatever can be possessed is not Dionysus. Therefore, the greatest danger for Nietzsche lies in wanting to incarnate Dionysus so as to at least be able to take possession of him in his incarnate form.[10]

On the basis of his theory of bipolar artistic forces, Nietzsche immediately emerges as a virtuoso in the art of an uneasy kind of self-reflection that does not believe its own observations. It does not believe itself, not because it has renounced itself or because it would abet a "totalizing critique of reason," but rather because the self of this reflection is constituted in itself (*an sich beschaffen*) in such a way that that which could allow it to believe in itself must always elude it. Nietzsche's dramatic thought is in the process of discovering that it is absolutely *impossible* for self-reflection and identity — in the sense of an experience of unity that could lead to contentment — to occur simultaneously. Whether as Apollo or as Dionysus, the named, identified, and masked subject is never permitted to believe that it has arrived at the foundation of its own identity. For as soon as it *sees* itself, this subject has already seen *through* itself as something wherein it cannot set its mind at ease because it is lacking the best part of itself, its Other.

Thus, Nietzsche's theatrical experience of self sets in motion a perfect system for self-disillusionment. Whatever might say "I" upon the stage will be a symbolically represented "I," an Apollonian artistic creation, which we hold out before us like a veil to protect ourselves from perishing of the complete truth.

Chapter 3
Cave Canem; or,
Danger, Terrible Truth!

*Lonely one, you are going the way to yourself. And your way
leads past yourself and your seven devils.*

Thus Spoke Zarathustra,
"On the Way of the Creator"

He who seeks a path toward himself is dreaming of a condition in which he will
be able to endure himself. For this reason, no search for the self can be a theoretical one, for this search arises from the impulse within the living being to find
a "truth" that will make his unendurable life endurable. Theorizing of any type
grinds to a halt when it reaches the level of radical questions of this kind, and
either leads to an art of living (*Lebenskunst*) or remains what it was — a symptom
of wounded life. The idea that the true self might be something that can indeed be
sought after arises directly from the suffering it causes. Only that which feels
pain begins to search — filled with the longing for a better self, which would be
the true one because it has ceased suffering on its own account (*an sich*). Thus,
only those who want to escape from themselves find themselves. It is the very
desire to escape that directly points to the direction of the path that the search for
self will follow. The search for oneself implies above all else the will to a path;
the direction that path will take can initially be none other than the path away
from oneself.

Embarking upon this path affords the wanderer the opportunity to encounter
his own shadow. Through the act of leaving, the wanderer begins to discover
what he has taken with him in spite of himself, just when he thought he had left
everything behind. The true self clings to the heels of the one who is embarking
on the path. But only when the wanderer realizes that he himself constitutes his
own heaviest baggage can the "dialectic of the path" begin. Through the efforts
made to flee, and also through the stimuli that accompany any meaningful
exodus, his powers increase to such an extent that he can recognize and endure

33

what, in leaving, he had not wanted to recognize and endure: the unendurable self. Only along the way does it become apparent how little of what the traveler has driven out of himself really allows itself to be shaken off. The more passionate his searching flight, the more vehement his realization of that which cannot be gotten rid of. Only the search that despairs of its own passion can arrive at the decisive point at which the search itself becomes as unbearable as what set it in motion. At this point, the agony of the search reaches its crisis point when it gains insight into the unattainability of what is being sought. The searcher must burn out (*verglühen*) when he senses that nothing will save him from himself. He is extinguished in the dilemma of having to choose between the unbearable and the impossible. Only in the fire of disillusionment can the last remaining illusions be burned away. With the departure of what is being sought, the search itself becomes the goal, and the path flows with a tragic bend into the pain from which it was initially able to turn away. *Partir, c'est mourir un peu*—that is how all paths begin. But *arriver, c'est mourir entièrement*.

The self-knowledge (*Selbsterkenntnis*) entrusted to the path of experience has, therefore, the structure of a negative circle in that it returns to its beginnings—that is, to its pain and its "love"—through the gradual repulsion of disillusioned ideas and the burning away of the images of happiness it had sought. This is, incidentally, completely different from the positive circle of narcissistic reflection, within which a seemingly material spirit loses itself and then rediscovers that identical self in order to perform, in the happy end, dances of jubilation around the golden idol of "I-have-myself" (*Ich-habe-mich-Selbst*).

I call this remarkably negative structure of self-knowledge the *psychonautical circle*; Nietzsche's theatrical adventure into the theory of knowledge is intrinsically implicated in it. His personal and philosophical fate depends to a great extent, I believe, on whether he can complete the task of burning away images and whether his search for self can be successfully completed within the context of a beneficial negativity and lack of representation. The risk involved in any such uncontrolled search is extraordinary; it can easily happen that the searcher becomes caught up halfway in a vision of his own ego, because of which he will announce, having been duped and enraptured, that this vision is what he has been seeking—*Ecce Homo*. Only a crisis will then reveal whether the seeker will plunge himself into a reflection in order to perish of its incarnation, or whether he will still have a chance to turn away from the mirror in order to assume responsibility for his life as a discovery that is void of images. But Nietzsche's drama is still far from arriving at this crisis point. He is still in the process of expanding the stage for his great play, exposing its antiquated foundation and properly determining what masks the actors will wear. Let us look at what else Nietzsche had in mind for his Hellenistic, psychodramatic stage!

Contrary to what might be expected, what appears there—after the intermezzo of his contemporary critique, the *Untimely Meditations*—is not a classically masked hero, not a Wagnerian tenor who has been transplanted into antiquity, and not a hero who has been transposed into modernity from the family of Oedipus, Siegfried, Heracles, and Prometheus. What we observe here is a figure who cannot be foreseen, who hardly seems to exist in a believable relationship to the tragic stage. What *is* produced there on the stage is a sort of theorizing Leporello, a freethinker and on-stage enlightener, who reminds us of the philosopher figures on the stages of the eighteenth century—of the Figaro in the works of Beaumarchais, perhaps, and even more of Don Alfonso in Mozart's *Così fan tutte* who, in his modish cynicism, has already mistaken the truth for a woman and woman for a synthesis of the bottomless cask and the thing "in itself" (*an sich*).

In the third trope of his self-objectification, Nietzsche reveals himself prima facie to be on paths that are anti-Dionysian. As I have already indicated, a critical activity that seems far removed from the mythological performances of the first scene results from his experience of himself within the Apollonian/Dionysian duality. Nietzsche now appears behind the mask of the philosophical specialist in abysses—also known as womanizers (*Weiberkenner*)—as the illusionless *grand seigneur* to whom nothing inhuman or human is alien. He speaks maliciously and with bravura of the lies told by the great men and of the abysses of the lesser ones; he presents himself as a virtuoso of cultural-critical distrust. He poses as a libertine underminer of idealistic values and as a positivist psychologist who, out of boredom with his own depth, makes fun of lending out to the British a dose of platitudes and to the French a prize for their infamous worldliness. Has Nietzsche thus completely turned his back on his classical and Wagnerian inspirations? The truth of the matter is that he acknowledged the Apollonian energy of resistance more openly in the psychocritical writing of his middle period. It is as if the rationalist in him were resisting subversion by the forces of Dionysus.

In order to appreciate the dramatic context of Nietzsche's maskings, however, one must first see lurking behind this third mask, which is negativistic and imposed by Apollo, a fourth mask—the mask of Dionysian prophecy. This is Zarathustra, drawn up to his full height, who will resound across the stage as the heroic tenor of immoralism, a subject his psychologizing precursor had only hinted at aphoristically, jeeringly, and in a miniaturizing way as an intellectual chamber play (*Kammerspiel*). It must therefore be understood that the masks of the third and fourth orders—here the Gay Scientist, there the prophet of immoralism—represent essentially only the unfoldings of the Apollonian and Dionysian double mask, from behind which Nietzsche's literary appearance had begun. The antagonism between the two artistic impulses within the soul thus remains every bit as valid as their relationship as accomplices—with the distinction that Nietzsche is now setting in *motion* what he initially presented within the context of a static symmetry and frozen dialectic. Within his process of thought, the polarity between the extremes begins to swing out of balance (*ausschwingen*)—all

Apollonian attempts at establishing control notwithstanding—and because of this oscillation, the Dionysian, which had been at first exhibited only as a dominated and silenced power, gains in latitude.

This is all just another way of expressing how closely this Nietzsche of the middle period—the one of the Gay Science and the great dismantling of values—is connected to the later Nietzsche, the one of the prophetic dithyrambs. The free-thinking, "cynical" underminer of all existing values—an Apollo who has turned malicious—remains the closest accomplice of Zarathustra, the Dionysus who has turned immoral. The all-penetrating psychologist of the stage performs, in his exercises in the critique of knowledge, the recitative to which Zarathustra's proclamation of self provides the aria.

In the thematic arrangement of *The Birth of Tragedy,* Nietzsche had already established the prerequisites for his next step forward. In the reciprocal distrust of both deities lay the philosophical dynamite of the future: the age of ideas was drawing to a close, while the age of energies[1] was announced. Radical doubt no longer leads—as is the case in Descartes—back to an unshakable foundation in the certainty of thought, but instead to a fireworks display of incredible reflection and a free play of doubting power. Doubt can no longer be assuaged in the certainty of ideas.

Nietzsche forges ahead unchecked on the trail (*auf der Spur*) of insights and hunches. He discovers while under way through the psychonautical circle that a labor of negation will be necessary that is as painful as it is invigorating. His gods experience a twilight from which they will never recover—the adoration vacillates, the brightly colored paper wrappings fall away from the ideals, leaving them naked and deserving only of laughter. Wagner becomes questionable to a degree from which he will not recover; Schopenhauer has retreated far into the background. Classical philology becomes completely nauseating, and the values of the new German present evoke only antipathy and contempt—the period of willful self-deception through the idea of a greatness of this sort has come irrevocably to an end. The exemplary seeker takes it upon himself to destroy, piece by piece, the value system, the world of images, the pantheon of the noblest goals under whose authority his exodus was set in motion. Nietzsche commented on this in retrospect:

> It is a war, but a war without powder and smoke, without bellicose attitudes, without pathos and dislocated limbs—this would all itself still be "idealism." One error after the other is put on ice, the ideal is not refuted—it *freezes to death* . . . Here, for instance, the idea of "genius" freezes; around the corner, the "saint" freezes. The "hero" is freezing beneath a thick icicle, and finally "belief" freezes, so-called conviction, even compassion cools down significantly—almost everywhere, the thing in itself [*das Ding an sich*] is freezing to death.[2]

No words could better express what it means to enter the phase of an active dis-illusionment. And yet Nietzsche's reflection remains too alert to settle down into a comfortable attitude of triumphal negation. The problem that will prove essen-tial has already emerged on the horizon: if ideals collapse, what becomes of the force that has motivated these ideals? After one is no longer able to deceive one-self, the question remains: what becomes of the impulse that has allowed one to deceive and lie to oneself? Nietzsche's thought advances to a level that corre-sponds to that of a thermodynamics of illusion; it orients itself, as it were, to a "principle [*Satz*] of the maintenance of illusion-creating energy." The idols col-lapse, and yet the idolatrizing force remains constant; ideals perish in the cold, and yet the fire of idealism continues to wander about, objectless and passion-ately desiring. The period of self-deception has ended, without the reservoirs from which the lies were supplied having been exhausted.

With this turning point, Nietzsche has begun to grow into a thinker whose thought will have incalculable long-range effects. Now we can understand why, when compared to Nietzsche's critique, all other forms of a critique of ideology seem short-winded and reveal themselves to be almost scandalously in want of a self-critical alertness. His realism thinks, as it were, a whole epoch ahead of itself. In his play with the masks of the deities of antiquity, he has already begun to gaze into the abyss of a self-doubt that cannot be assuaged, from which arose the phenomenon of the fundamental untenability of reflexive subjects. What he gained from this is as disturbing as it is entertaining—his insight into the exis-tential inevitability of the lie. One can imagine what would become of philoso-phy if this conjectured insight were to prove true! To a much greater extent, one is *not* able to imagine it!

The compulsion to lie has its base in the nature of truth itself—as the young Nietzsche presumes to define it with the unabashed confessional willingness of the unbroken genius, as well as with the relaxed receptivity of a man who con-siders it a distinction to be a student of an important intellect, Schopenhauer. But what is this truth, part of whose fundamental nature it is to make us lie? Nietz-sche says it plainly: the truth lies in primordial pain (*Urschmerz*), which has im-posed the fact of individuation on each life. Using the expression "primordial pain" in the singular is in any case paradoxical, since there are as many centers of primordial pain as there are individuals. To be condemned to individuality is the most painful of all pains; as regards human subjects it is at the same time the truest of all truths. If, however, "truth" means primordial pain for the individual who has been "thrown" into being (*ins Dasein geworfen*), then it is in its specific nature to signify insufferability for us. We are therefore able to want not to rec-ognize it at all—and if we do surmise anything at all of it in its immediateness, we do so only because the veil of pretense and representation that usually conceals it has been opportunely pulled back, so that we, racked with pain, suddenly understand more than will do us good.

This would mean that the known forms of the "search for truth," especially those of the philosophers, the metaphysicians, and the religious are, in reality, only organized lies that have become respectable and institutionalized attempts to escape that have disguised themselves behind the diligent mask of the desire for knowledge. What had previously pretended to be a path toward truth was in reality a single thrust away from it, a thrust away from what was unbearable into the provisory tolerability of comfort, security, edification, and transcendent worlds. After Nietzsche, it is almost impossible to overlook the fact that most previous philosophy was nothing more than an ontological whitewashing. With its whole pathos of loyalty to the truth, it committed an act of betrayal—as necessary as it was deplorable—of the unbearable truth, to the benefit of a metaphysical optimism and those fantasies of redemption that project themselves into the beyond.

If, however, truth is not something that can be be sought, and if any search for it is defined *in advance* as terrifying, intellectual candor finds itself in a position it had not expected to be in. Truth no longer reveals itself—if it reveals itself at all—to the seeker and the researcher, who actually want to elude it, but instead to him who exhibits the deliberateness and courage required to *not* seek it. To be sure, how he exhibits these qualities of courage and deliberateness remains his secret, and it is certainly conceivable that enough will always remain from the search for truth as is necessary for the search for deliberateness and courage, without which a nonseeking consciousness could not develop. He who does not seek the truth must believe himself capable of enduring it. All problems of truth are therefore ultimately confluent with the question of how to endure what is unendurable. Perhaps this is why there are ultimately no techniques for finding truth in the existential sense; in the labyrinth, one looks not for secure knowledge but for the way out.

One may not therefore dismiss Nietzsche's entreaties of heroism, courage, and tragic wisdom as mere manifestations of pompous self-stylization and the mannerisms of masculinity, regardless of the extent to which the latter do in fact play into his habitus. Courage is necessary within Nietzsche's enlightenment, primarily for taking part in the phenomena of truth (*Wahrheitsgeschehen*), because, for him, it is no longer a matter of a game of hide-and-seek, but one of experimentation and constancy, which remains, if possible, in the vicinity of the terrible truth. For this reason (according to Nietzsche), anyone who wants to speak of truth without using quotation marks would have to first prove himself as a nonseeker, a nonescapist, a nonmetaphysician.

With the acknowledgment of primordial pain as the basis of all other bases, Nietzsche's early thought places itself under a tragic, theatrical, and psychological sign (*Zeichen*). If truth means the unendurable, then knowledge of truth cannot be abruptly defined as enduring the unendurable. It is that which is unendurable itself that forces us, incircumstantially, to maintain an unwavering distance from it. Accordingly, the truth about the terrible truth is this: we must always have just missed it, and, furthermore, we will never be able to have the sincere volition (*Willen*) to recognize it in its relentless presence (*Präsenz*). For we are able to want only what we can still endure. According to Nietzsche, knowledge of the truth therefore also means always having been placed at a protective distance from what is unbearable.

Distance — that is the key word in the new tragic theory of knowledge, after which the old optimistic theory of the desire for unity was at an end. Philosophers, seekers, and dreamers might therefore continue to speak of identity and unity, but the thinkers of the future, the psychologists, know better. Their thematic is that of distance, duality, difference. He who knows about distance has made the optics of a philosophical psychology his own. The psychologist also knows that he is enduring just as little of the whole truth as anyone else, but through this knowledge he gains a point of orientation toward which the general theater of self-deception and liar's play of life can be referred. The psychologist is well aware that everything is merely theater: through his personal union with the tragic theoretician of knowledge, he also knows, however, that it would make no sense to want to close this theater in the name of truth. Indeed, the terrible truth is the mother of theater. In accordance with its nature, we maintain an irrevocable distance from it, a distance that so radically determines our everyday existence in the world that, even with the staunchest will to truth, we are not at liberty to distance ourselves from this condition of distance. As a rule, it is impossible to survive the final dissolution of the distance that exists between us and the unimaginable reality of the terrible truth. Nietzsche's phrase "We have art in order not to die of the truth" can also be read in this way: we maintain a distance from truth so that we will not have to experience it directly. To speak ontologically, art — the old veilmaker — has us in order to in turn protect us from having the truth.

There can be no doubt here: wearing the mask of the theoretician of knowledge, Nietzsche has made an unprecedented appearance on the stage of philosophy. Do we now understand that this was no longer philology — and never was? Do we recognize how something new and unbounded has taken shape within this philosophical project (*Aktion*) — something new as pertains to truth as the oldest liar, whose wealth of discoveries is not exhausted as long as life itself attends to anything unbearable that might want to save itself in the liar's theater of inventions and research along the brink of the unbearable? Do we appreciate what ramifications the idea of distance will have? If it is indeed valid, then our position vis-à-vis truth (independent of all our conceits of seeking and finding) must be one of an unavoidable evasiveness and a distance from which we cannot distance ourselves. If the terrible truth always keeps us at a distance, we are no longer able ever simply to "grasp" it. Whatever we may say *about* it, it is no longer actually *there* in what is being said. We can therefore no longer succumb to the illusion that a condition of living without illusions is possible for us. We are condemned to simulation by truth itself. For us, illusion would be the most appropriate way to conduct ourselves toward the terrible truth. We would grasp the truth only in that we have already eluded it as far as possible.

All of this will bring forth unimaginable ramifications, since the possibility of our ever fully expressing the truth henceforth becomes a chimera. The terrible truth does indeed precede all assertions, but this preexistence does not mean that the former could be "expressed" or represented in the latter in the way in which the idea is expressed in the symbol or the object in the sign (*Zeichen*). The terrible truth is in everything we express and represent, but it is no longer *present;* it is not this terrible truth that guarantees the truth-value of individual assertions. This could be formulated as follows: from this point on, any assertion remains, as it were, alone. Representations have been abandoned by what they allegedly represent—the truth—and must rely on themselves without the sanction of the final authority. The "whole truth" no longer plays along; it is no longer there in its supposed representations. Thus the signs remain unto themselves—relying on nothing but their own internal relationships, their own system, their own grammar, their own "world."

With this, the catastrophe of signs that have been abandoned by the "whole" truth is initiated, a catastrophe that is bitter, but also stimulating. The first character to carry out the prospects and the risks involved in the ambivalent disaster across the stage in an affirmative way will be called Zarathustra. It is no coincidence that this herald of immoralism is at the same time a rediscoverer of prophetic speech. *Thus Spoke Zarathustra* is, in my opinion, an experiment based on the possibility of theater after the end of the "representation" of truth on stage, an experiment that has not been thought out to its conclusion to this day. It is the first hypothesis on the possibility of an absolute play in the form of unprotected pure self-expression; it is the incarnation of the transition from plays that represent to those that present, and an exercise in the semantics of godforsakenness, that is, in speaking in the absence of the "truth." Zarathustra's manipulation of language (*Wortergreifung*) is like a sound that has been transcribed into a linguistic music that, in its notes, carries out a fervent revenge on everything that could hinder the resounding of his voice. It is, so to speak, a nihilism that has become music, or a melody that has become immoralism; it would no longer permit any court in the world to either allow or forbid its ringing out and, relying only on the small autonomy of its real sounding, will submit itself to no foreign or external standard. Zarathustra's song is the daring self-staging of the Dionysian release from restraints (*Enthemmungen*) that bursts forth on the stage as the unprotected self-affirmation of a language. That Nietzsche also disguises himself as the Antichrist and presents himself as someone who will save us from morality—the embodiment of all the lies we have endured—should be seen in this light, not as the expression of an extravagant overestimation of self, but as part of a stringent logic that governs a new understanding of art and truth. For in order to be allowed to show, in a self-affirming way, what he is or what he wants to be, the frenetic and unprotected representer of self must overthrow what was previously known as culture—the entire system of altruistic and dualistic values with its poisonous cargo of restraints, self-reification, and self-negating impulses.

Interpretation is unavoidable here; if what Nietzsche says about the truth is right, there would then be two truths—one terrible, which drives us along ahead of it by dint of its unendurability, and one endurable, which surrounds us as necessary illusion and as life-enhancing benefactor. As something that is necessary, this illusion (*Schein*) has retained a strange ontological dignity and imperviousness— it also retains an ultimate transparency toward bad things that are unimaginable, but is not absorbed into this transparency. The "illusion" therefore cannot be reduced to truth, and there is no longer in any way, as there has been throughout the entire tradition of metaphysics, the "illusion" of a "being"—although even now, what is unbearable in the world precedes the bearable illusion. For all that, it does not impair the self-will of what is bearable. The illusion subsequently becomes autonomous and necessary a posteriori. What more would it need to flourish?

Only now does the impact upon philosophy of what had come into the world in the form of *The Birth of Tragedy* become apparent. Anyone who might not have deciphered it from Nietzsche's awkward and precocious expositions on the composition of the chorus would ultimately have it forced upon him by the subsequent development of the motif. For what the ancient chorus—this self-entranced mass of sound that no longer *represents* Dionysus, but *is* Dionysus—had wanted to indicate is expressed directly and affirmatively in Nietzsche's aesthetic-metaphysical work, and especially in the presentation of Zarathustra—to wit, to hell with deeper meanings! To hell with higher truths! Let's call a halt to the idea of the preexistence of meaning with respect to its expression! Long live the signifier! Long live noise and smoke! Long live the sound and the image! Long live the illusion of the autonomous symbol, the absolute dramatic representation! Meaning, truths, abysses, gods—they must tend to themselves from now on. We will no longer concern ourselves with them, because everything we are meant to concern ourselves with must be illusion: endurability, perspicuity, conceivability (*Vorstellbarkeit*), image, sound, body, stimulation, contiguity, demeanor, taste.

It is enough to open one's eyes. Where are the unbearable truths? In this instance, a life-dispensing distance separates us from them, and if we look directly ahead of us and lend an attentive ear to the present, we will see and hear the physically present illusion in its relative endurability. We will be able to do this to an even greater extent if art should occur in our presence, if choruses sing or if

Zarathustra allows his word-music to resound: "From out of an never-ending abundance of light and depth of happiness it falls, drop for drop and word for word—a tender languor is the tempo of this speech." What blossoms forth here is an intermediate world of sounds and surfaces, not merely bearable but actually inspiring, whose presence conceals the abyss of the terrible truth. It is only a matter of dwelling on the interplay of signs and sensualities and of not sinking into trying to imagine something that is absent—as theoreticians and those who are absentminded do unremittingly. If, as it seems, the principal truth of primordial pain itself brings about a world of bearable secondary truths, we can hold on to the latter as long as we are able to succeed in not thinking about "it," and do not break out of cheerful observation into speculation. Accordingly, we may neither remember primordial pain abstractly nor anticipate its return imaginatively. Whatever was, and will be again, must take care of itself in its own good time. But he who seeks to get a grasp on neither the pain of birth nor that of death and thus lets the matter of the unbearable and the unimaginable drop—he can discover before him, with no further ado, an intermediate world made up of sensual presences. The average human destiny is fulfilled in this—and *only* in this—in-between or intermediate world (Nietzsche uses this expression in *The Birth of Tragedy* for the Olympian sphere). And yet, in this intermediate world, the penultimate is perceived as the ultimate, and the tentative as the conclusive. It exists because man engages in the ephemeral as if it were the permanent. The blossom of the intermediate world is art, which in rare instances can ascend to the level of the tragic, a type of art that itself is the highest form of philosophy. Within it, the illusion of the illusion has become reflexive, and betrays itself, at a dizzying height, as a happy lie and as the most genuine deception. Nothing comes closer to the truth than whenever the beautiful places itself as a fragile, endurable thing before the *foundation* of the unbearable. "If philosophy is art . . . ," then, to paraphrase Heidegger, it is the art of existing in an endurable way, of being exempted from the unendurable.

Thus, the idea of scrutinizing oneself in the process of the play of aesthetics becomes one of the points of junction in Nietzsche's philosophical perception. The phenomenon of art as the living manifestation of lying, image-creating, inventive energy offers an enticing opportunity for the self-objectification of a life that is compelled to seek. For it may be that individuals with a deep wound and a great sense of compulsion, even though there is no chance of their occupying a defined form of self-existence and finding comfort in a specific mask, are still free to experience themselves within the context of their own aesthetic efforts and to say to themselves, At least in that which I can reveal of myself as an artist I can leave behind my own truth, the truth of myself, even if it might soon be superseded and forgotten. I no longer need to have any doubt, at least in what the course taken by the storm of the production of myself has exposed of me, and even if it were true that I, like all individuated life, am only a plunge from the unbearable into the unbearable, here, at this point in the course of the plunge, I am enduring myself as best I can. I am with myself, and I no longer have to skeptically undermine the fact of my being real as a knowing mask. *Fingo ergo sum.*

There is thus still so much invested in the most unstable self-production that it has placed itself in the world once and for all as a fragment of a real illusion. Through it, the aesthetic subject gains, through the vortex of self-doubt, its first—and perhaps only—foretaste of an irreducible existence that is superior to any penetration. There *is* something there; it can see itself and it can be seen. It can even, semiempirically in its own defense, accept itself and validate itself. The world could collapse without any doubt having to arise in what pure self-perception called to the artist at the instance of his expenditure: This is what I was! That happened to me! I was necessary in achieving this effect! It may not be of much use as a work of art—but whatever speaks in it spoke through me! I may be ephemeral, but my ephemerality is negated in what became real through my participation in an artistic phenomenon.

Whatever Nietzsche addresses, the movement of his self-awareness is bound to the tracer path (*Leuchtspur*) of his great literary publications. In that it is actually he who objectifies himself, mask for mask, he begins to exert upon himself a powerful allure of self-seduction—as if he wanted to persuade himself to finally declare himself found. After all, what ultimately looked back at him from the mirror was no longer a short-winded philologist or an intellectually dependent devotee of Schopenhauer and Wagner, but the image of a man who believed that he had reason to look upon himself as a genius and a philosophizing "destiny." The author of *The Gay Science,* the poet of Zarathustra, the first psychologist of his time, the reassessor of all values; what Nietzsche had before him as his objectified self was in reality nothing parenthetical! Yet what is it that seduces him into plunging into his own image, like Narcissus, in order to drown in himself?

There can be no doubt that the daring presenter of himself also had a chance, even at the dangerous heights at which his performance of self was enacted, to withdraw from his masks and let them remain as ephemeral countenances, that is, as transitory incarnations of a potential. No search is programmed a priori as a flight from pain into madness—provided the thinking actor understands his own play as a play and sufficiently draws on the commitment of life to what can be endured. In this way he could carry his "psychonautical circle" to its conclusion and burn the last deadly phantoms of the divine incarnation behind him. Actually, in his post-Zarathustrian period (whenever his compulsion to suffer gave way), Nietzsche sometimes comes very close to an amorphous tranquillity—at least until the images finally deluge and devastate him.

With this, our dramaturgical meditation on Nietzsche's metamorphoses comes to a critical point. Which "mask" would be left for the thinker on the stage after he played himself out to the very limit of what could be incarnated in the tortuously sublime figure of Zarathustra? Where would he find the gestures of a post-Zarathustrian playfulness? How would he elevate his impossible prophetic exhibition through a fifth masking, and make the attempt to incarnate immoralistically in Dionysus something he could survive? Is not a denial the only thing that remains after a theatrical explosion of this kind, whether it be in the form of a retreat into madness, a resignation into silence, or a metamorphosis into the wise fool? Nietzsche captured with his characteristic precision his experience of the self in the difficult position of a Zarathustra who has left the stage without having a new role:

> Except for these ten days of work [a reference to the enthusiastic days spent in writing *Zarathustra*—Au.], the years during and above all *after Zarathustra* were a disaster without equal. One pays dearly for the privilege of being immortal; one dies many times during one's own lifetime to make up for it. There is something I call the "rancor" of greatness: everything great, whether a work or a deed, turns, once it has been accomplished, against him who has accomplished it. Precisely because of the fact that he has accomplished it, he is now *weak*—he can no longer endure his own accomplishment, he can no longer look it in the face. To have something *behind* one that one never could have wanted, something that will be bound up in the fate of humanity—to now have it *upon* oneself! . . . It almost crushes one to death . . . the rancor of greatness! (*KSA* 6, pp. 342–43)

Is not the plot of the drama also laid open here? This unhappy compulsion to see behind what he himself is doing? This incessant doubling of the self into what is spontaneous and what is remembered? This despairing undertaking—the attempt to take possession of himself as the incarnation of the most grandiose of self-representations? This is indeed the "rancor of greatness"—that it is compelled, through its greatness, to suffocate that which wants to reunite it with its ego. What cannot be questioned is that Nietzsche experienced himself often enough in authentic medial terms; he knew the resignation of doubt and an almost somnambulistic constancy in the articulation of his powers.

But his inherent makeup undid the liberating effect of such experiences time and time again; what repeatedly prevailed was the subsequent ego-centered (*ichhaft*) self-assessment of nonegotistical creative processes. Thus, Nietzsche constantly doubled himself into the praise giver and the recipient of that praise; in spite of all his psychological wisdom, he consistently fell back into the posture of one who felt it necessary either to be praised and valued by others or, for lack of recognition, to sing his own praises. Because of this, he remained condemned to exploit himself permanently and to capitalize eternally on his own vitality and intellectual power. His new ideas were consistently devoured by the oldest structure of values, and the dead ego's compulsion toward self-assessment always prevailed at the expense of any vital efforts. As long as he remained trapped within this structure of self-assessment, he was far from freeing himself from the terror of values — under these circumstances, even a "reassessment of all values" provided no release. The point of crisis occurs when it becomes apparent that an incarnation of the gods is more likely than a "twilight of the idols." It is more likely that the subject will flay itself to death as the raw material for a revaluation of self than that its value system will release it. Nietzsche's structure is predetermined in favor of a suffering grandiosity that creates value; in having to decide between existential happiness and value-creating greatness, this structure as it exists within him always chooses that which, at the cost of a terrible self-sacrifice, serves the process of the creation of values.[3]

I believe the complex of ideas that was involved in developing Nietzsche's theorem of the will to power can best be understood by bearing the foregoing in mind. Perhaps it is a bad habit within the field of Nietzsche research and an example of the most dangerous type of carelessness that its scholars specialize in either the earlier or the later Nietzsche and interpret the aphorisms on the will to power as representing his fundamental philosophical teaching — especially since we now know that this "major work" is counterfeit, having been compiled by Nietzsche's sister, Elisabeth. In contrast to this, we must insist that the early Nietzsche was correct in his assessment of the most important matters in a way that the later Nietzsche was not. And as often as it has also been noted that the Nietzsche of *Zarathustra* and *The Will to Power* is much closer to the Nietzsche of *The Birth of Tragedy* than the Nietzsche of the middle period, who presented himself as a playactor of positivism, this proximity has for the most part never been properly related back to Nietzsche's prototypes of truth (*Wahrheitsmodelle*) at the beginning and end of his philosophical career. A joining of this beginning and end reveals that the tenets of the will to power represent positive versions (*Positivierungen*) — as dubious as they are desperate — of the negative model we have read in *The Birth of Tragedy*. The earlier prototype of truth ("the unbearable inflicts upon us the compulsion toward art") was, on its path toward a suspect metaphysics of energetic egotism, transformed into an affirmative one, divested of its memory of the dialectics of the unbearable, and paraphrased into the later prototype of truth: "The will to power establishes a life-enhancing illusion."

Even for the early Nietzsche, life, viewed *sub specie artis,* is essentially a composing (*dichtend*) self-representation, whose movement struggles away from the unendurable toward what can be endured, and suggests both a volition and a compulsion toward art. Hence, the will to art appears — thanks to a constitutive mystification — in its own interests (*für sich selbst*) as the primary element. For purposes of critical reflection, however, it is recognizable as the secondary, subsequent element precisely because it is grounded in the self-veiling of the unendurable. We are only indirectly aware of what we are unable to endure as such in the form of traces of memory that the catastrophe of individuation has left behind within us, or in the shuddering contemplation of the convulsions of those who take the secret of their immediate encounter with the unendurable with them when they perish. For this reason, the will to illusion in no way originates in and of itself, but is grounded in a compulsion toward illusion. But when we hear the theorem of the will to power, our recollection of this more complex structure seems to have been obliterated in an almost ingenious way. Nietzsche's later thought allows the will to power to ascend to the highest rank and any previous urgency to disappear in the fact of will.[4]

In this, Nietzsche'a basic aesthetic-ontological hypotheses are initially plausible. If individuated life is essentially a composing of self-representation above a foundation of painful pleasure (*Schmerzlust*) and impulsiveness, then one can certainly be of the opinion that the universal concert to a great extent is composed of the noise of these compositions of self, which resound against each other and are dependent on each other. Since life is already compelled to art because it has been afflicted with individuation, it must discover within itself the yearning that the philosopher identifies as a will to power and that more than anything signifies the will to implement one's own true lie of life and art at the expense of others. Even if this process were to function in this way, the will to power would still have been preestablished in a compulsion toward the will to power. Certainly, no vital composition of self can exist without a will toward its own realization; still, the (active) composition of self as such is based on a compulsion toward composition (*Dichtenmüssen*) and a faculty for composition (*Dichtenkönnen*) that precedes all volition.

Now we can see how Nietzsche deviates from his earlier insight vis-à-vis subjectivity and the metaphysics of volition. If life is self-composition, then the will to power is only one of its possible exegeses—and probably not the fundamental one, for a faculty (*Können*) must precede any volition. Thus the axiom of the will to power seems plausible only to those who have in mind a sort of social Darwinism with Hobbesian undertones that has been transposed into the realm of aesthetics—as it were, in the form of an artistic struggle of all against all with the final survival of the fittest. That Nietzsche himself operated with such hallucinations of an absolute polemics (having been influenced by, not least of all, Darwin, who was his contemporary) need not be demonstrated. In truth, however, the self-composing structure of life can develop optimally only once it has taken possession of a faculty. By this I mean that the will to power is a perversion of the right to strength. Wherever a will to power is proposed as the ultimate wisdom, the subject already mistrusts his own power to compose himself, and attempts to think himself into safety by means of the application of will. A will to power need not be presupposed as long as the right to strength is confident in itself.

We have already indicated the extent to which an inability to believe in his own self actuated Nietzsche's logical mechanism. Whenever strength feels its release obstructed by a surplus of restrictive counterforce, it must want to maintain itself all that much more in its remaining expression. Its intention to be itself has at its base not the structure of a will to power but that of a will toward being *able* to want, which suggests nothing other than the phantasm of the restoration of naive, uninterrupted, unfettered strength, which *can* to the same extent that it *may* and — occasionally — *wants*. Probably Nietzsche's most serious psychological and philosophical error was displacing will from the status of the occasional to that of the fundamental.[5]

Accordingly, the construction of the will to power betrayed itself as a symptom of excessively restricted strength — a situation that is by no means equivalent to weakness but, quite the contrary, suggests strength with a bad conscience. It is an energy that has not grown into its condition of restraint. For this reason, it wants — hungry for a release from restraint — to speak freely of itself through an immoralistic act of unleashing, certainly not in order to leave the door open to malice as such, but so as to be able to applaud an absolute expression of strength. It is hardly necessary to state that this applause has been inspired by a utopia of the innocence of the body, a utopia in which the traumas (*Traumata*) of the civilizing process register their protest. It is impossible not to overhear in this the voice of a wounded life — and in this it is dialectically interconnected, as revolt, with a destiny of oppression. It is, like every "kynical" (*kynisch*) act, a contribution on the part of immoralism to the success of life, which must release from the soul a whole world of moral restraints and wrongs — and to this end also engages in volition and provocations.

I would suggest that Nietzsche's tenets that pertain to the will to power be understood primarily as a subjective reclaiming of older quasi-fundamental ontological insights and, second, that this reclaiming be integrated into the psychodrama of the thinker as an act of Dionysian "kynicism" (*Kynismus*). The will to power is, in my view, not a "metaphysical" thesis that should be read in the indicative, but a hypothetical dramaturgical pose. Its truth-value cannot be discussed in terms of a "final statement," but only as that of an intellectual dose to be administered in the midst of a crisis of strength. Contrary to Heidegger, I would not read Nietzsche's corresponding statements on the subject as representing without exception the termination of European metaphysics in an active nihilism, however seductive this master interpretation may be. It is suggestive as an interpretation of individual lines of thought in Nietzsche's work, but its plausibility collapses as we look more closely at the dramatic tangle of Nietzsche's games of reflection. The will to power: I read it as a self-therapeutic and, if you will, allopathic prescription, which pursues the fundamental ontological motif of tranquillity by means of a radically subjective jargon. For the essence of the volition of the will to power indicates something that would lead away from the will: it "wills" tranquillity in the sense of an ability to entrust oneself to the limitations of one's life and in the sense of permitting oneself to let go, which in turn leads to the pure intelligent ability to be. But in order to permit what he wants, he needs—having become malevolent through experience—the protective armament of a sovereignty that would no longer feel compelled to defer to judgments and restraints.

Only because of this, Zarathustra must proclaim the ethos of liberation from all the old authorities with the intonation of a neoauthoritarian. Because Nietzsche cannot trust his own ability to compose himself, he must appear as the legislator of freedom from the law. His energy is expended almost entirely in declaring its unrestrained permission to expend itself. One can sum up the dramatic mechanism behind Nietzsche's appearance in the mask of the Antichrist in this single statement: "I want to be permitted." This desire for permission, however, is only the parody of an ability that must already be present for a long time before a volition can be activated. Because the condition of having to want is behind this volition, volition and compulsion belong within the same sphere of nonfreedom. Perhaps Nietzsche, because of his tenacious insistence on the will, is unable to experience how a liberating "You are able to" would anticipate his "I want to." Like most of the moralists of the modern era, he has failed to appreciate that the origins of justice lie in permission—that is, the acceptance of a great abundance—and not in prohibition, as a narrow-minded dialectics would have it, and also not in the proprietary appropriateness of a decisive establishment of values that will be the determining factor in Nietzsche's immoralistic concept of justice. (I will return to this theme in Chapter 5.) Any attitude that maintains an attitude of "I want to be permitted" inevitably remains the inversion of "You may not." The rebellious will neglects experience in order to relinquish itself to a struggle-free ability to exist beyond subjugation and revolt. The experience of being upheld by a legitimate authority suggests nothing else. At the same time, this would be the experience of a self-love that is neither aggressive nor meek, and which admits that a love has accommodated it. These experiences have only one thing in common: they do not allow themselves to be induced by volition. For Nietzsche, however, all that remained in this sphere was the attitude of standing firm in the face of an almost fatal state of deprivation.

Of course, tranquillity is never achieved through a will to tranquillity. If the composition of self prefers to take place behind the protective shield of a self-betraying will to power, then the self-expression of he who is composing himself is not released but rather ensnared in the paroxysms of a forced spontaneity. If impudence elevates itself to the level of a principle—thus falsely Platonizing itself—then opinions will burst forth that are merely allegories of impertinence, and that signify anything but this self, in the positive sense of the word. Nietzsche knew this as well: "We always find ourselves, in the initial stages of all vices, so very near to virtue!" No one understood better than this, the gentlest of immoralists, that virtue is at the root of every vice. In him, his "superrefinement" (to use Lou Andreas-Salomé's expression) was at the root of an allegorical brutality. As the will to malice, impudence must become the parody of a divinely naive unaffectedness that flutters before all efforts to achieve effortlessness.

Nietzsche's audience will view his final performance with great anxiety. They observe a man who will have to entrust his last insights to his failure. From now on, observing him will be painful. Anyone who, like this author, is compelled on principle to want a fundamental ruthlessness merely to expose the space in which he could come to "himself" appears as someone who is about to fall apart. An active nihilism offers only a terrible substitute for a man's ability to remain on friendly terms with himself. The revolt may not, in any case, be substantiated. Through his frantic proclamation of egotism as the reversal of the centuries-old lies of altruism, the thinker risked *himself,* becoming the battleground for a ruthless battle of principles in which his own well-being could play only a minor role, as had been true in the oldest altruistic violations. In that Nietzsche produced allegories of egotism from himself (*aus sich*) with increasing vehemence, he forgot the minimum of legitimate egotism that would have been necessary to render his terrible astuteness endurable for the poor animal behind the masks. Through the efforts of his will toward egotism, Nietzsche neglected to accept himself as a being who, without the support of a principle and on the basis of his own preexisting nature, had already always had permission to be egotistical. He wanted to transfer what had been conceded and allowed all along into something self-willed—perhaps so as to no longer rely on anything except the isolation of all good spirits. Did he not in this way venture too near to the terrible truth?

In his finale, Nietzsche proclaimed the unprecedented freedoms, the most extreme releases from restraint, the ultimate intensifications. And yet no one responded to him; the thinker remained alone with his paradox, and his freedom was tantamount to a metaphysical punishment. Like a Bajazzo of egotism, he ascended from his isolation in order to take the stage, and presented to his audience the gift of freedom, which he himself had taken but never actually received. Perhaps his greatness lay in the fact that he gave what he himself lacked, and his undoing in the fact that he never received as a gift what he wanted to pass on to others. Against his will, he was the last altruist.

Chapter 4
Dionysus Meets Diogenes; or,
The Adventures of the Embodied
Intellect

> *You shall create a higher body, a movement, a self-propelled wheel.*
>
> *Thus Spoke Zarathustra,*
> "On Child and Marriage"

The construction of the tragic stage in *The Birth of Tragedy,* as we have suggested, was in itself a preparation for the appearance of Zarathustra. The Nietzsche of the early 1870s, however, was as little aware of this as his contemporary readers were. What he did sense very clearly, though, was that the first tremor of a philosophical earthquake had been registered in this book. Bearing this in mind, what did the resistance of his colleagues and the silence of his profession signify? Even the masquerade of Apollo and Dionysus would have seemed only a matter of secondary importance in the face of this tremor. For what the young Nietzsche had set in motion by positioning in the wings of the tragic stage a spectator named Socrates—who represented a whole universe of wayward philosophizing—would soon prove more important than what was apparently taking place on the stage itself. It seemed almost as if Nietzsche wanted to supply evidence in support of the tenet that all decisive blows were dealt with the left hand—or, to express it better, that the real dramas were being acted out along the edges of the stage.

I will attempt—with an occasional subversion of the text—to retell the play within the play, and to tell it in such a way that a three-dimensional image of the dramatic process emerges.

What is happening? On his way across the tragic stage of art, Nietzsche experienced *nolens volens* that, in the festival performances named after Dionysus, Dionysus himself is no longer a match for the Apollonian compulsion to symbolize. Certainly, the magic spell of tragedy depends on the cultlike chanting of the he-goats; and yet one aspect of the matter is also that a he-goat who can do nothing but chant eventually cuts a tragic figure. Were there not, before there was music, truer ecstasies and more impervious raptures that had fallen victim to the Doric process of precensorship? Would the god of intoxication acquiesce to such curtailments? Would he not be compelled to fly into a rage over this aesthetic swindle of sacrifice? Had not the form his revenge would take already been predetermined by destiny?

An unobstrusive figure appears in the wings of the theater. His name is Socrates—but we should caution the reader that this is a pseudonym, or at least not the man's full name. This figure indicates no understanding for the sublimity of the play, and does not take part in the artistic intoxication of the others. He sits there—he fidgets back and forth, shakes his head, and yawns. Sometimes he even speaks out loud in between, spontaneously offering theoretical suggestions on the progression of the plot. According to him, the heroes would not have to unavoidably perish if only they could keep this or that in mind. By God! Could it be that a philosopher has lost his way and wandered into a tragic theater? The strange visitor behaves loathsomely. And yet, during the terrible convolutions of the hero's agony, he exhibits the most malicious optimism, and always seems to want to say: It doesn't have to be this way; things could be otherwise; destiny doesn't follow a fixed script—we ought to let something other than this occur to us! The true disciple of Dionysus can only turn away in disgust from so much insincerity. Whoever is so lacking in good taste that he does not take life seriously as a tragedy cannot be proper company for a well-schooled Dionysian. Or can it be that he *is* proper company precisely because of this?

Nonetheless, the most resolute partisan of tragedy will not deny that a Dionysian pleasure must complement Dionysian pain—indeed, not only complement it, but constitute and surpass it. The fact that this pleasure hides behind the masks of optimism and comfort would correspond completely to the abysmal superficiality that one must credit to the playful god of intoxication. Is it not part of the essence of tragedy that it is reflected in comedy? Does not the pain want to vanish so that pleasure can stake its own claim to eternity?

In any case, the Dionysian (*Dionysiker*)—or should one say fan of Dionysus (*Dionysianer*)?—is alarmed. He knows there is someone in the audience whom he must dismiss as contemptible at first glance, but whom he also cannot afford to let out of his sight; his presence has something unsettling about it. Perhaps he is an unforeseen incarnation of a god? He looks like an idiot, a tramp, like a reasoning ape—but who can know for sure? Perhaps he is a cunning mask of a god, which would lead us to conclude that he is a smiling god? From his smiles, deities have sprung forth; from his tears have sprung forth men—so goes the myth. On the other hand, one never imagined that the laughter of a god could be so insipid. This guy always laughs at the wrong moment; he laughs off the mark, he speaks when he shouldn't, he sits where he shouldn't—and he understands nothing of the dramas of individuation, nothing of the metaphysical convolutions of heroes, and nothing of the murderous violence inherent in the dilemmas. For if he did understand, how could he still laugh? If he were prepared to unite in compassion with the god, how could he then abandon himself to his vulgar gaiety, rubbing his belly and, under the open sky of the tragic stage, reduce the deity to a good man?

All of this notwithstanding, the shallow buffoon hangs about obstinately in the retinue of the deity. The only thing that can be noted to his credit is that he does not allow himself to be thrown off by any of the contempt shown toward him. He avoids all questions as to what he is looking for here or whether he belongs there at all with an ironic wink, as if he does not quite comprehend what the words "look for" or "belong" mean. The more sublime things become, the more idiotic his laughter sounds. The more ceremoniously the symbols are spread out, the more energetically he shakes his ugly head and makes counterproposals in the face of destiny! Is he not a stain on the magnificent vestments of Dionysus?

But maybe he also has something to do with the terrible truth of the god — perhaps it is his embarrassing mission to favor the mediocre over the profound? Perhaps he has been given the terrible duty of informing us that the truth is really *not* so terrible after all. We would then have to concede that Dionysus was not the most terrible of all deities because his terror is not absolute. A god in whom we sincerely want to believe should at least not be ironic: Dionysus is up to no good with the sincere believers among his followers.

One of the greatest intuitions contained in Nietzsche's first book is revealed by its coupling of the dramatic resusitation of tragic wisdom with the birth of the Gay Science — even if this is done in a very enigmatic and imperceptible way. The intrinsic polarity Nietzsche treats in his book is precisely *not* that between the Apollonian and the Dionysian; the dramatic theme of the book is the relationship between the tragic and the nontragic. An attentive reader must be astonished by how easily the compromise between the two deities of art is accomplished by Nietzsche the philologist, while, on the other hand, he has considerable difficulty removing the world of tragic art from the world of nonart, of mundanity, of rationality and theoretical behavior — in a word, from what he terms Socratic culture. Nietzsche required no more than a few pages at the beginning of *The Birth of Tragedy* for the compromise between Apollo and Dionysus. For the balancing of the tragic with the nontragic, he needed the rest of his life — without ever finding a solution to this lamentable complex. In the course of his efforts vis-à-vis the nontragic, however, he became a genius of dedramatization, of cheering up, and of taking it easy. Thus the same man who, while wearing the mask of the Antichrist, vented his emotions in the form of highly charged pathetic outbursts, also became one of the founding fathers of the Gay Science.

As Nietzsche interprets them, Apollo and Dionysus harmonize so splendidly that their historic compromise could be synonymous with a form of "more advanced'' culture—Freud's theory of culture and neurosis is really only the continuation of the Nietzschean concept of compromise. However, Dionysus, the embodiment of divine vitality, cannot bear to be honored exclusively at the altars of this more advanced culture. All along, he has also laid claim to the wild side, and is therefore also called the god ''to come'' (*kommend*), not least of all because he is as thrilling as sexual ecstasy, which is the most ''*kommend*'' experience that human beings know. His domain is the wilderness of intoxication, to the extent that this also represents a vital experience for human beings *within culture*; culture is possible only if that which is older than it and supports it remains preserved within it. And yet the term ''wilderness'' for Dionysus suggests more than a music reservation administered by Apollo. For this reason he does not, if he is honest, like to attend operas, and the tragedies that are supposedly about him are more likely to inspire him to yawn than to give him pleasure.

It may therefore be the case that this laughing and yawning idiot whom Nietzsche sees emerging at the edge of the tragic stage is in truth a messenger of the god to come, who is supposed to make it clear to his solemnly high-strung followers that he is from time to time in need of more palpable forms of adoration. If tragedy will be forever only an orgy in place of an orgy, this fact will ultimately prove to be an argument against tragedy—no matter how sympathetic we are to the advantages to be gained from the substitution. In order to punish, but also to caution, the friends of tragedy, Dionysus resolves to give them the initiative to come to their senses through a messenger whom they will in all likelihood not believe—so that they will most certainly miss the god behind the pretext of his cult: they would then possess the unmisleading sense for the masked truths Nietzsche substantiated.

Do we now understand the immeasurable consequences that must result from the introduction of this philsophizing spectator? Through his introduction—as banal as he may seem at first glance—the Dionysian phenomenon, which was initially only postulated and which had been put on ice by the forces of Apollo, could be set in motion in an unforeseen manner! The petrified wrestling match between Apollo and Dionysus could be transformed back into a vital struggle— provided the Dionysian front was no longer acknowledged as existing only in the tragic spectacle, but also, and above all, in the discrete play of the nontragic.

As a result, one would have to decipher the scene—which consists of a chorus, heroes, the public, and the philosopher—differently than has been customary up until now. Certainly, the god would appear, as Nietzsche shows, further objectified and illustrated by Apollo, and at the same time as a dream image of the chorus, as the suffering hero on the tragic stage. But what if he were also to appear, unillustrated (*unveranschaulicht*), within the audience itself in the guise of a vulgar philosophizing fool, who makes fun of the heroes, the tragedies, and the whole world of the symbolic? What if Dionysus were no longer alone in his futile assault on the Apollonian impulses of representation? Perhaps he could, while he waltzes across the orchestra pit in the convulsions of his dilemma, also sit in the balcony and enjoy the spectacle he is making; perhaps this blasphemous amusement signifies the essential and most consequential breakthrough on the part of the Dionysian through the fissure of culture. Because Dionysus has denounced the absence of a divine wilderness in the innermost region of culture, does he not, more than anyone else, have the right to sneer at its symbolizations? Only the god of the theater can dare to ask, What is the point of theater?

These statements, which go beyond Nietzsche's text—and may seem to disregard it—are essential for bringing the phenomenon that is unspecified but inherent in the text into a proper light. For when Nietzsche supplements his thoughts on tragedy with those on nontragedy—of course, he does this reluctantly and in open conflict with his tragic-heroic élan—he is preparing the way for the insight that, in the future, we will have to reckon with a twofold manifestation of the Dionysian: a higher one and a lower one, one that is symbolic and one that is pantomimic, one that is celebratory and one which is commonplace, one spectacular and one imperceptible.

Anyone who is serious about the Dionysian cannot overlook the fact that, in addition to the great music festivals of universal transfiguration, there must also exist Dionysians of the commonplace—if this god really does mean to signify the essence of the reality of the world differently and to represent not merely an impresario for week-long Dionysian cultural celebrations or an excuse for artistic stimulation under the supervision of Apollo. Musical festivals of universal ecstasy, from Pergamum to Bayreuth—why not? But can the Dionysian calendar be satisfied with only two weeks of festivities? Is the always approaching (*kommende*) god sufficiently honored by one debauch per year? And even if it is true that a year-long orgy would be a contradiction in itself, and that it is part of the fundamental structure of the festival to whirl past in great cycles—the truth of the god must be preserved and shown respect in an appropriate manner during the periods of his absence. The orgies cannot become chronic, but the truth of the orgy—this absorption of the individual consciousness into an enraptured nonobjectivity that releases it from the misery of individuation—can and must also be elevated to the status of an unpretentious keepsake. More than anyone, Nietzsche has again put us on the trail to the proper name of this keepsake: for two thousand five hundred years it has been known as *philosophy*.

It is unbelievable: as long as it has existed, philosophy has—with a few suspect exceptions—presented itself as the opposite of all that which the most ordinary understanding would define as the Dionysian. From the very beginning it has presented itself in a favorable light as tranquillity itself, seeking the cheerfulness of the spirit, and existing only in the higher realm of ideas. And now it is suggested that philosophy is fundamentally a manifestation of the Dionysian, appearing incognito as something unobstrusive, hermetic, and far removed from tragedy. The plausibility of this suggestion stands and falls with that of these initial assumptions: that there must necessarily be Dionysians of the commonplace; that the truth of Dionysus also knows a nontragic means for manifesting itself; and that therefore a suspension of consciousness has developed that deciphers the arrival of the god in the thousand ordinary things that, because of their everyday occurrence among us, make up what we refer to as the world.

Assuming that this is all true, it is obvious why the philosophical thought that had become scholastic had to have experienced great difficulty in defining itself from the very beginning—because it has ever since been communicated best whenever it has itself forgotten that for which it had originally stood. In Nietzsche's *Birth of Tragedy,* the veil is pulled back a bit from the mystery for the first time. Accordingly, the Dionysian calm after the storm appears as the authentic philosophy. It is the celebration of the commonplace in the light of excess; a haze of postorgiastic thoughtfulness therefore surrounds all original thought. The ecstasy vanishes, order returns once again, and the everyday resumes its course. But the astonishment remains. The elevated universal experience or universal fusion of intoxication has an obscure aftereffect. Somewhere—should we say, within?—the Dionysian fissure gapes open like an abyss or a nothingness into which everything that comes along will henceforth sink like something monstrous, even if it is the most unobtrusive and commonplace.

In its most pedantic manifestation, however, philosophy would not consider thinking of itself in this way. Soon after its debut, it had already involved itself in an undertaking all its own. It soon forgot that it had initially been one half of a bipartite cultural wonder, which led on the one hand to the birth of tragedy out of the spirit of the musical orgy, and on the other to the birth of philosophy out of the spirit of difficulty, which was to be carried out in the interim between orgies. Since then, philosophy has turned a deaf ear whenever it has been in a position to hear the truth about itself; it does not want to acknowledge that it is a mode of thought that is in a state of remembrance of orgies past[1]—an orgy in place of an orgy, a drama in place of a drama. Like every chronic search, it one day put itself in the place of what it was seeking and thereby lost itself, seemingly self-satisfied, in the contemplation of higher realms of thought and spiritual hidden worlds, intelligible structures and logical procedures. What would later be called "metaphysics" developed through this substitution; "theory" developed through the repression of the Dionysian consciousness of universal arrival (*Weltankunftsbewusstsein*) by the objectifying and stagnant worldview; both have left a very deep impression on the history of the West. In both, the dominion of a "truth" is announced, the consequences of which seem incalculable.[2]

Nietzsche was the first to recognize that the word "truth" was almost always, in the language of philosophy, the equivalent of "substitute," "alibi," "pretext," "surrogate," and "representation." He saw through the illusion of the "real world" as a surrogate world, and through the "true" knowledge of the philosophers as a knowledge in place of knowledge. Philosophical truth was for him always a "truth" that stands in place of something else. What is true within the truth therefore cannot possibly be understood without a theory of substitution and representation (*Stellvertretung*). Once again we encounter Nietzsche's great subject of illusion; once again we observe the interplay between an affirmative illusion that places value on its impenetrability, and a residue of transparency that makes it possible to think from now on within the context of a critical function. For if the substitute were not, to a certain extent, just as good as or better than what it was replacing, it could not replace it. If it did not stand in its place, we would always have to be dealing with something that could not be substituted for—we would always be immersed in the mute thing in and of itself and would not be able to maintain any distance from it. Thus, it would seem to lie in the nature of the substitution that it places a substitute before itself, through which we can apapt ourselves to it. What cannot be replaced herein reveals its affinity with the unendurable.

What does this have to do with philosophy? Naturally, these surrogate Dionysians, who have established themselves as hard-hearted lovers of knowledge, belong in some way to the Dionysian phenomenon because they could not replace it otherwise. They acquire their critical distance to the real Dionysians "first and foremost," however, in that they sense nothing of their own surrogate-Dionysian quality and have since the time of Socrates found themselves in the position of being oblivious to Dionysus. And yet, if Dionysus is also the god of the surrogate Dionysians, then a Dionysian fundamental phenomenon must take place in the Dionysian oblivion of theoretical thought. And accordingly, Dionysus also prevails in the *modus* of his withdrawal, his absence, his oblivion. Only in the twilight hours of thought and within the framework of epochal ruptures in intellectual history does Dionysus awaken, as it were, to himself and become a more reasoning mode of thought—a condition of alertness inspired by dangers, which no longer represents anything but is rather the unmediated self-contemplation of the monstrous.

Does this suggest merely a variation on Heidegger's thought, which has not yet decided between parody and paraphrase? One would have to say instead that Heidegger has transposed Nietzsche's parody of philosophy into an unauthorized melancholic key. There is everything to indicate that this time the farce preceded the melancholic version and that Heidegger's parody of Nietzsche is a more serious offense against the rules of art than the droll original. It is a parody in place of a parody—when philosophy was in its infancy, who would have thought that it would someday bring forth something like this? But there should be no panic among Heidegger's adoring multitudes! That *The Birth of Tragedy* can be read as we have read it already presupposes the alternatives (*Möglichkeiten*) that Heidegger's earnest thinking out has won by means of Nietzsche's impulse to criticize philosophy, and the dramaturgical freedom we have assumed in our reading of *The Gay Science* is one of which Heidegger was the coconqueror. Nietzsche's playfulness becomes evident only in contrast to Heidegger's seriousness. But what permeates the seriousness and jocularity is an epochal mutation of consciousness, the consequences of which become immeasurable once Nietzsche has entered his postmetaphysical period—a mutation that cuts like a century-long awakening into an era of thought and that counteracts its dramatic future. He who is lucky enough to be able, because of the modest organization of his intellect, to dismiss this as mere irrationalism should stay asleep for a while longer—but an unusual task awaits those who have awakened early.

This task begins with this still-painful denunciation of Socrates that gapes forth in Nietzsche's book like an open wound. Nietzsche disguises himself here as a freethinker well schooled in the best tradition of the Enlightenment who is striking down a father of the church with the momentum of his anticlerical fury. Socrates, the father of the theoretical truth! Socrates, the archdogmatist of human self-improvement through mere reason! Socrates, the intellectual mixer of poisons and demon of a negative enlightenment! Socrates, the unmusical barbarian of thought who, in his furor of reason, no longer conceives of tragedy as a misfortune but rather as a "problem," and who no longer understands that life is above all else a process of self-composition—and not an object for self-reflexive deconstruction! With him, the decline of tragic consciousness begins, and philosophy enters into an age of theoretical optimism, a term that is merely another name for the most insipid Dionysian obliviousness.

Listen to the tone of these reproaches! Nietzsche is not protesting against the abrupt invasion of the scientific intellect into Greek thought, which occurred in the brief interim between the appearance of Socrates and the work of Aristotle. He objects to the un-Dionysian, unartistic, theoretical self-misrepresentation of philosophy in the persons of those who—after Heraclitus—are its greatest representatives! He does not intend to forgive Socrates for having destroyed the unity of art and philosophy that had lent its depth to an older way of thinking and was informed by Dionysus, and which could be rediscovered in a new way of thinking. *The Birth of Tragedy* therefore does not limit itself to an anti-Socratic tirade, and certainly not to a mere denunciation of philosophy. In publishing his book, Nietzsche intended to point the way to a future potential of an art-enriched thought that has been reborn through the spirit of Dionysus. *Ecce philosophus! Dionysus philosophos!*

In this early book, Nietzsche has already initiated a radical restylization of the philosophical intellect. Even in his great reprimand of Socrates, his intention is to save the thinker from his merely theoretical obsession. "If philosophy is art . . . "; if the philosopher is possibly only a clever he-goat in a state of postorgiastic meditation, then the concerns of Dionysus are not lost theoretically. Two alternatives are available, through which the he-goat could dispense with his theoretical horns—Nietzsche has taken both into consideration. The theoretical Socrates could be rehabilitated through Dionysus as a "music-making" or as a "raving" Socrates.

The first path had already been offered to the ancient Socrates, if the legend is correct, by his demon—who this time spoke to him not to dissuade him, as he usually did, but to challenge him: "Socrates, make music!"[3] For Nietzsche, this meant that a philosopher could be forgiven for anything except for being musically deficient. However, to the extent that Socrates represented the incarnation of a concept-weaving unmusicality, he really did lead philosophy in a direction that was unforgivable. Nietzsche does not, however, view this false step as irreversible. Had not Schopenhauer, in his metaphysics of music, already broken through the wall that divided the philosophical universe from the musical one? Was not Wagner a living example of the fact that it was possible to unite the genius of music with the tragically ideal in earlier doctrines of truth? And, above all else, was not Nietzsche himself already involved in testing a new union of the divided spheres?

As far as the "raving" Socrates was concerned (a figure who would assume a significance as great as it was clandestine in Nietzsche's later writing), he need only read what Diogenes hawked to Laertius in his *Lives and Thoughts of the Famous Philosophers* through his namesake from Sinope. Here we read *Sokrates mainomenos;* the phrase was coined by no less than Plato. And what could be read beyond this—a collection of anecdotes on a capricious, malicious, life-drenched doctrine of wisdom that refused to constitute a philosophy—was enough to offer Nietzsche, the artist-theoretician who despaired of theoretical thought, advice he should never forget. This would all point to the trace of the almost physical untheoretical spirituality of the character type that was Dionysian, and yet nontragic.

In future writings, Nietzsche will mention his ancient source only with an averted gaze. Only with the protection of a psychological and moralistic incognito can he succeed in following the ancient trail (*Spur*) and in profiting from it—to a degree that would exceed anything imaginable.[4] "Something cynical, perhaps; something 'weighty' " (*KSA*, 2, p. 375) will now come into play in all of his works.

Nietzsche's discretion here is easy to understand. By openly establishing a connection with the irreverent bravura of the "cynical writers" (he refers to them, as we will recall, in *The Birth of Tragedy* in the course of his criticism of the Platonic dialogue as the equivalent of the novel form for ideas), he would have disavowed his stance of tragic, aristocratic self-stylization, in which he—the eternal royal child (*Königskind*)—had invested so much. He would have had to make two admissions at once, when the one—that there was a nontragic manifestation of the Dionysian—was already difficult enough. He only succeeded in making the second admission right at the very end: he admitted that there might also be a plebeian form of greatness. For, in spite of everything, there appeared within the earliest form of "kynicism" an indespicable plebeian gallantry as the *amor fati* of the poor scoundrel—indeed, as in *Crates*, there appears in poverty as a chosen way of life a rare sovereignty. More than any individual detail, there is a wild sense for the price of freedom, and he would experience the denunciation of the lies of comfort and the beautiful antics of the middle path. In the primary representations of "kynicism," an impressive denial of the authority of man-made laws is revealed—expressed in the decision to submit himself without cultural trimmings to the majesty of the *physis*. Here the term *physis* does not mean the paragon of the object world or the gearwork of an obdurate cosmic causality; it is to a much greater extent the guarantor of an existence that does not defer to any reification, and is thus esteemed as the physical foundation of ecstasy, of which the freedom speeches of the philosophers communicate only the diluted infusion. The ancient speech of *physis* was not a tyrannically objectifying cult of physicalism, but rather a ways and means through which the consciousness of a hermeneutic *gnosis* of the body could express itself.

All of this had too much in common with Nietzsche's own philosophical and psychological tendencies to have eluded him for long. Indeed, "kynicism"—together with certain rudimentary elements within the stoical Heraclitic movement—was the last and most anonymous form of ancient doctrines of wisdom, and thus of a form of thought that conforms to the play of forces and the dissonant consonance of *physis,* without losing itself in the phantasms of philosophical doctrines of the beyond. Let the depraved ghosts worry about transcendence and spin out their "relationship" with immance! The consciousness of the ecstatic physicists (*Physiker*) refuses to ascend into the transcendent worlds of the philosophers because for them there exists no transcendence that remains within *physis* and that values it highly enough. He who wanted to establish a postmetaphysical mode of thought, as Nietzsche undertook to do in the strongest moments of his thought and in his whole literary guerrilla war on the great truths—he had to take up the trail of the last premetaphysicians, especially if he was to prove that he was a Greek scholar who had read his Laertius better than anyone else.

But what does it mean to take up the trail of a consciousness that, because it lacks the will to theory and does not believe in the vital significance of speculation, has left hardly a trace behind it? What constitutes the trail of this consciousness, which has disappeared almost without a trace? Surely not these few statements by the "kynics" on the cosmos as the home of man or on nature as the measure of action? Presuming even the slightest standard for a theoretically developed capacity to question, these statements must be found lacking. The dominion of "kynicism" lies elsewhere—in its habitus, its mood, its infatuation with the current, in its *style*. This oscillates wherever it is authentically reembo-

James E. Cheek
Learning Resources Center
Shaw University

died, between didactic pantomime and satirical "checkered writing"—satyr plays of the body and the pen. Thus the concept of literature comes into play here for the second time with a specific emphasis. Again, Nietzsche violates the rules of his profession with his brightly checkered literarization of philosophy, no differently than the way in which he had, during his initial appearance on stage, already strayed from the framework of what was permissible within the context of philology. It was precisely in doing this that he—somewhat surreptitiously, but also with a decisiveness that leaves no room for any doubt—takes up the thread of that which has stretched from the "cynical writers" of antiquity through countless entanglements into modernity.

The Gay Science begins to spin its vestments from this thread; it will soon openly speak its name in the title of a subsequent book. It will speak first with the best kynical psychologizing of the "human, all-too-human," of the petty, malignant truths of the commonplace that the blind gaze of theoretical sight has already overlooked. Without literature, no truth; without psychology, no alertness; without "cynicism," no freedom to call things by their names.

And yet one should not delude oneself about the status of Nietzsche's psychology. However much it flirts with the perspective of the natural sciences and the stupidity of British positivism; however much it purports to flee into the Apollonian and plays out the role of a cold presence of mind in the face of former ecstasies, this psychology has, at its impulsive core, a long since been not a theoretical undertaking but instead a *dramatic* one. It organizes Dionysians of civility, and excesses of disillusionment. Dionysus *cool*. Nietzsche wrote in retrospect:

> But he who is related to me by the *height* of desire thereby experiences
> the true ecstasies of learning. . . . There is absolutely no prouder and at
> the same refined type of book . . . here and there they achieve the
> height of what can be achieved on earth, cynicism: one has to conquer
> them with the most tender fingers as well as with the bravest fists.
> (*KSA*, 6, p. 302)

It is the same Dionysian impulse that gives the author an unparalleled understanding of the psychodramatic tissue of ancient tragedy and, at the same time, opens his eyes to the Dionysians of the commonplace, the satyr plays of the banal, and the circles of hell of the all-too-human. As an aesthetician as well as a psychologist, Nietzsche becomes the mouthpiece of a consequential Dionysian invasion of the theoretical and moralistic culture of modern bourgeois society.

It is true that, in his twofold presence as orgy participant and psychologist, as Dionysian hero and critical rogue, Nietzsche brings to light a character who is anything but straightforward. He is *modern,* with all the implications of that term, and as such does not omit the self-contradiction and ambivalence that belong to modernism. He is *decadent;* a man who has been seriously wounded by culture, in all its resultant ramifications — the most valuable of which appear openly unequivocal with time. As E. M. Cioran has correctly observed, "His *misere* was therapeutic for us; he opened up the era of complexes."[5] His was, indeed, a "serious case," and yet nothing could prevent him from discovering in himself deeper reserves of healthiness than anyone would have credited him with, considering his wound. His laughter was unfounded; the experience of his life did not justify it. Perhaps because of this he was authorized as no one else had been to state that pleasure — even within the context of sorely tested existence — was a deeper phenomenon than pain. In any case, he had, as overserious intellect, discovered something that was uncomplicated within a condition of complexity — a halcyon cheerfulness with which he veiled the news of the terrible truth. Cheerfulness is the courtesy of the complex.[6]

Even now, the Gay Science is still the most polite way to openly discuss the unbearable elements of existence. There is no way to retaliate against the clever idiots who, because of the light tone of the work, conclude that the thought contained therein is in itself insipid — except with the beautiful statement with which Nietzsche has characterized the relationship between the philosopher and those among his public who are merely clever and inexperienced:

> Every deep thinker fears being understood more than he fears being misunderstood. The latter wounds his vanity, perhaps, but the former wounds his heart, his sense of compassion, which always responds, "Ah, why do the likes of *you* want to suffer as I do?" (*KSA*, 5, p. 234–35)

Nietzsche paid a high price for discovering that Dionysus not only manifests himself as a suffering hero and an ecstatic chorus, but can also plunge into the human fray as a psychologist, itinerant mystic, accursed philosopher, and stylist. When he escaped into the nonidealistic, he lost the sympathies of the Wagnerians, and thus let fall the most important external supports for his confident self-awareness.

Anyone who studies Nietzsche's inner conflicts during the period of his separation from the cult of Wagner and from the constraints of the academic chair in Basel will find it hard to avoid speaking of a social death, a categorical existential and philosophical separation. For those who have entered into the psychonauttical circle, a social death is inevitable. Only it can bring to an end the interplay between the collective and the personal lies of life, which unite so gladly around common values: I praise you, you praise me — we both lie. But he who is experiencing a social death because he has begun to find himself can no longer be helped by anything general or by any external encouragement. Whoever believes that he is engaged in real thought without having first peered into the abyss of his own singularity is merely trying to convince himself that he is thinking — he

dreams a conformist's dream, and wishes it were the dream of a critical consciousness. He who really thinks is condemned to an isolation that compels him
to begin anew and to fulfill himself; henceforth, there will no longer be any "tradition," but only a rediscovery of himself in affinities and constellations.

During his "kynical," psychologizing, knowledge-criticizing years, Nietzsche forged ahead into an isolation that was constitutive of a mode of thought
oriented toward the terrible truth. Only through the discovery of a positive and
liberating isolation could the pleasurable-painful (*lustschmerzlich*) prophecy of
the Dionysian psychocritique free itself from its involvement in the idealistic
fraud of the Wagner cult. Because isolation exonerated him from all considerations, Nietzsche was quickly able to free himself from the false classicist mannerisms that still cling to his book on tragedy. Redemption from the idols created
space for the implementation of harder, purer values. From now on, it was a
matter of Voltaire versus Wagner, romantic *esprit* versus a deep-rooted Teutonic
clumsiness, the freethinker versus the religious fanatic, a serene nihilism versus
a neoidealist self-indulgence in higher worlds, the malicious tongue versus a
beautiful foaming at the mouth, the shadowless phenomena of the south versus
the northern lights of cynicism, the "cynical" music of *Carmen* versus Wagner's
oppressive Venusberg, the truth of the small energetic stab versus the lie of great
style.

One thing cannot be denied: Nietzsche was profound in his descent into the
isolation of his new precision. From this point on we have known more about the
consanguinity of cruelty and profundity, but also more about that of the precision
of good humor—the precision *nota bene* of musicians and artists, not of administrators of knowledge and those who count mistakes, who confuse devotion to
their inhibitions with precision.

He who shoots off theorems like arrows and gives out bites like statements must
believe that he can rely on what he is saying having an effect on the pain/pleasure
scale, *index veri,* for the author as well as for the public. Nietzsche practiced this
belief as only a true believer can; his *credo* demanded that there should be no
pronouncements of truth without consequences—and if these consisted of the
perishing of the perceiver because of that through which his will to truth had
overextended itself: *fiat veritas, pereat vita.* This outlook on the possible adversity inherent in the correspondence between knowledge and effect explains why
Nietzsche's *credo* suggests more than merely an overblown artist's concern for
effect, and certainly not a reduction of philosophy to rhetoric.

Nietzsche's concept of style is based on a condensation of all speech into the
pleasurable/painful physical foundation of knowledge. In his pronouncements on
truth, the truth itself begins to become concrete—not in Lenin's sense, which
ultimately confused truth with grenades and allowed its concreteness to atrophy
into a strategic brutality called "praxis." Rather, it is concrete in the sense of a

somatic aesthetic—a return of the true into what can be perceived as true, a renewed and deepened investigation of knowledge and sensuality. Nietzsche's writing provides the prototype for a modern philosophical orality. What increasingly takes the upper hand in his pronouncements on truth is, in addition to the musical character of his lecture in general, the bittersweet pleasure he finds in taking the world into his mouth (*In-den-Mund-Nehmen der Welt*) as something he both loves and hates; the wild joy in biting and being bitten without which the Dionysians of this divination would not possess a physical foundation in the body. One can also say that, in Nietzsche, the sense of taste once again takes on a philosophical dimension as the most intimate of the universal senses. Philosophy reaches back into its somatic sources; the world is initially experienced through the mouth.

For this reason, Nietzsche's critique of knowledge and psychology—particularly that of the middle period—does not comprise a soul-soothing theory, even though it does borrow from the grammatical structure and philosophical vocabulary of such a theory. His "theory" is an oral guerrilla campaign (*guerilla*). It is true that his philosophical, psychocritical writings are presented in a glittering Apollonian prose that, with its malicious simplicity, feigns contempt for any merely theoretical complexity. But these writings, with their forced rationalism and positivistic petulance, should be read as oral Dionyses in miniature. They are the bites, screams, and leaps—transformed into language—of a psyche compelled to communicate its cool state of delirium alongside the constant arrival (*Ankunft*) of the world.

Nietzsche is trying out a way of speaking that gushes forth from the speaker so quickly, so precisely, so dryly, so calculatedly, and so fatally that, for a moment, the difference between life and speech seems to have disappeared. In the moments of the highest oral intensity, that which is said is consumed in the act of saying it; all representations are reduced to ashes in the act of being expressed. There are no longer any semantics, only gesticulations; no longer any ideas, only tropes of energy; no longer any higher meaning, only temporal stimulation; no *logos*, only orality. There is no longer anything holy, only heartbeats; no longer any spirit, only breath; no longer a god, only the movements of a mouth.[7]

Who can wonder at the fact that, up until this day, this language has been in search of those who understand it? It is the language of the postmetaphyical human being, and perhaps only a sort of children's language as well—a return to a joyful orality at the heights of culture?

A hundred years after Nietzsche, it now and again seems as if an almost popular coming to terms with this singular philosopher were possible. Perhaps a majority of the aesthetic successes and the important philosophical self-representations of the present day are only the fulfillment of what was announced in his work. One indication of this among countless many is the excessive corroboration that

Nietzsche's verdict on the "cynical" *Carmen* has found among the mass public today. In addition, we could also count the return of opera, the renaissance of pathos, the discovery of a second misfortune (*Fatalität*), a general obsession with the physical, the wholesale renunciation of finalistic apparitions, the irresistible privileging of taste over ethics, and the unnerving vacillation of souls between isolation and consolidation (*Vereinnahmung*), between the effort to separate and the desire to unify, between the hell of difference and that of identity. All of these are Nietzsche's landscapes, and we inhabit these landscapes, not because we "also" share his problems, but because his problems and the language in which he deals with them increasingly guide and overshadow our own problematizing.

Taste instead of ethics—where will it lead? What is taste, anyway? How can such an unfathomable quantity take on meaning in intellectual terms? And what if this is not the proper way to phrase the question? What if all systems of signification (*Bedeutungswelten*) have always been merely systems of taste—different ways and means of translating the aroma of the world into linguistic articulations? Could it not be that all metaphysical doctrines have only served to coat the bitter pill of life in the sweet confection of an assigned meaning? "And you tell me, friends, that there is no disputing of taste and tasting? But all of life is a dispute of taste and tasting" (*Thus Spoke Zarathustra*, "On Those Who Are Sublime").[8] Have not all the great methods for organizing the world been merely manipulations of taste (it is no coincidence that the words "cosmology" and "cosmetics" have the same root), and all philosophical statements only perfumed attempts to stifle the unbearable fumes of the universal sewer in the effort involved in conceptualization? Psychology tells us that taste is the most intimate, the most universal sense of perception, and Heidegger tells us that moods explain the world. The preacher Salomonis went into greater detail: woman is bitter, he said, and Nietzsche shared in this taste—without questioning the authority of his biblical predecessor.

Nietzsche's exceptional position among the modern philosophical authors is grounded above all, in my opinion, on the fact that, like almost no other thinker before him, he focused his reflections exclusively on the interplay between mood and taste. He was a philosophizing stylist because he consciously adapted his writing to the *modi* of orality. Speaking with an extraordinary intensity of moods, keys, variations of taste, levels of volume and *tempi,* he was the first philosopher to grasp that language *itself,* style *itself,* and expression *itself* were nothing other than lifeless pseudo-Platonisms, from which the remains of life were fleeing. As a consequence, the expression of truth in itself came to a halt for him. *How* truths were expressed was from then on their own affair, and was relative to the mood (*Stimmung*) of the instrument upon which they were played—the excitable body. The reverse side of this insight would read as follows: Eliminate the excitability of the body, and you will win *one* "truth."

Wearing the mask of Zarathustra, Nietzsche was the one who, as the first modernist and without having been a Sufi, came upon a truth that wanted to be danced. He was also the one who knew that truth could be expressed in laughter. A truth-through-tears (*Wahr-Weinen*) had also confided in him in moments of Dionysian emotion, without taking into consideration the soldier in him, who preferred to find the truth contained in "holding fast" and standing his ground. And what could be said about the "truth-through-vomiting" (*Wahr-Kotzen*) that presented itself as an accompanying symptom of the severe migrain headaches that plagued the flayed body of the writer who had so little flair for lying?

Nietzsche developed two modes for expressing the truth to a greater extent than any of the others: truth-through-biting (*Wahr-Beissen*) and truth-through-singing (*Wahr-Singen*), both of which are the ultimate stagings of an oral truth that has been mediated by taste and mood. Truth-through-biting is the prototypical gesture of a psychological writing of the "kynical" type of unmasking, which oscillates between a biting to death that causes him to suffer—whether through obtrusiveness ("The cattle among my friends, mere Germans, by your leave . . . ") or through deprivation (did he not refer to Lou Salome, after the "disappointment," as that "withered, dirty, foul-smelling little ape, with her false tits"?)—and the desirously precise, cruel and tender nibbling at subjects with which mere contemplation would accomplish nothing in the face of a sensual hunger for knowledge. Nietzsche knew truth-through-singing as a gesture that legitimately appeared with anyone who had learned, through great suffering, to cherish the value of good moments. "Singing is for those who are convalescing; the healthy man prefers to speak."[9] A man who had to bite through entire worlds of constraints and deficiencies—a man who was too sensitive, who wanted too much, but who was also like an eternal convalescent, so happy to be able to celebrate in song a few great recoveries, Nietzsche exercised in his work a body of writing that brought to light, between the small bite and the great *melos,* between laconism and the dithyramb, an unmistakable individuality.

This wonderfully mobile and well-trained body of language executed "leaps and handstands" (letter of January 25, 1882), which even today could not be performed by anyone who was theoretically motionless and on ice, even if he published fat-bodied theories of aesthetic experience. But Nietzsche's capers would be fundamentally misrepresented if we were to see in them only vigorous asides to serious questions of truth. In them was manifested—precisely as it was in his flights of pathos—a Dionysian subversion of the *esprit de serieux,* with which the modern world, with its theoretical and moralistic dominions of sentiment, is leadenly weighed down. In his physicality of language (*Sprachkörperlichkeit*), he wanted to announce a new ethics (Phooey! But do we still react this way today?) of thought. Nietzsche's holy lesson in behavior is recommended as would be a hygienic or dietetic measure—as a sort of intellectual and spiritual musical training, as a mental gymnastics course for practicing a new pyschophysical ethics of intensity. Nietzsche knew that there was nothing more improper than a lack of energy that appears disguised as a science. He sensed that there was nothing more suspect than a fear of the truth that passed itself off as a critical consciousness, and nothing more perverse than an inability to recognize that which confused itself with circumspection. Above all, Nietzsche developed a thoroughly volatile sense for the obscenity of the so-called communication of subjects who are not sufficiently daring in how they express themselves; how he hated the phenomenon which George Grosz later caricatured in his *Republican Automatons*—these functionaries of their own selves, these display-window mannequins of their own essence! He uncovered the vampirism inherent not only in the Christian ethic but, to an even greater extent, in that of a moralistic-theo-retical culture.

I am certain that, in the long run, this will prove to be the more important of Nietzsche's reassessments of values. The "unmasking" of Christianity as a movement of *ressentiment* and as an epochal deadly assault may prove insignif-icant when compared to the uncovering of the physicality of thought. This is not a mode of thought that concentrates *on* the body, and not a playing-off of the physical against the intellectual; rather, it is a *physical* intellectuality in which the drama of a postmetaphysics appears. Therefore it is always an intelligence "on the verge" of something—an intelligence in transit, on stage, in the mood. It does not cling to the subject as if it were private property, but thrusts it forward like a provocation and a revelation. Perhaps in this context the limitations of the old dumbstruck Enlightenment will become blindingly (*blitzhaft*) clear as repre-senting those of an attempt to limit intelligence like an active subjective property to a defined center of a static, risk-free character, instead of an understanding that comes into play only as a dramatic and procedural quantity—beyond the illusion of the propertied individual that has distorted every aspect of life in modernity. Nietzsche recognized intelligence as the virtue of the wanderer and "psycho-naut," and as a component at work in the makeup of the seafarer, of whom he wrote:

> Indeed, we philosophers and "free spirits" feel, when we hear the news
> that "the old god is dead," as if a new dawn shone on us; our heart
> overflows with gratitude, amazement, premonitions, expectation. At
> long last the horizon appears free to us again, even if it should not be
> bright; at long last our ships may venture out again, venture out to face
> any danger; all the daring of the lover of knowledge is permitted again;
> the sea, *our* sea, lies open again; perhaps there has never yet been such
> an "open sea."[10]

In each of these cases, it is a way of thinking that, in its fundamental concepts and basic operations, still utilizes dramatic categories—no, it is a phenomenon that can only still fulfill itself in categories that exist because of their analogy to drama. *Tragoedia facta est quod philosophia fuit.* Within this dramaturgy of the spirit, no statements are valid, only scenes; no "ideas," only plot lines; no discourses, only provocations. Thinking is the phenomenon of thought: the adventure of the perceiver, the drama of dramas.

Nietzsche encircles this phenomenal cleverness with a ring of sparkling metaphors: metaphors of sea journeys, tightrope walking, flight; alpine or nomadic metaphors; metaphors of fragrance, sound, trembling, and surging—metaphors of gushing forth, rupturing, rolling forth from oneself, overflowing, ejaculation and parturition. All of these images reveal a phenomenal intellect that is searching, creative, testing in nature—a *logos polytropos,* which signifies nothing other than a brightness (*Helle-Sein*) of the body on its great journey out of the earth and around the world.

It is most important to stress here that, in Nietzsche—as in all postmetaphysians of the Dionysian type in general—it is never a matter of organizing a compensatory justice. We cannot permit ourselves to be caught up in Nietzsche's rhetoric on this point: his self-awareness of his creation of epochs did not have real historical-philosophical significance. What this author is doing does not constitute a pure enthronement of sensuality, which was supposed to be helped back to its proper place after the theoretical ascetic excesses of the Western *ratio.* Postmetaphysical reflection is not intended to be a balancing mechanism against an excess of anything—something intelligible as opposed to something sensitive (*Sensible*). It is also not a new beginning after something has ended, such as the return of the body after an era of disembodiment has run its course, and it is also not the sunrise of great honesty after an age of hypocrisy.

What is it then, if it is not any of these? It is the constantly self-accomplishing deepening of subjectivity of the universally open in the body's process of becoming more linguistic and more universally yielding, which is enriched in the course of its conscientious composition of self with increases in cohesion. Does this mean that the relationship between body and intellect has been reversed—seemingly contrary to all metaphysical principles? In the place of *logos* being made flesh, it would seem that now *physis* has become language. But even this formulation is incorrect, for this does not occur in its place, but rather becomes apparent as the fundamental phenomenon that, from time immemorial, has also encompassed the "word becoming flesh!" The process of the *physis* becoming illuminated and lingual is much older than the descent of *logos* into the body—both older and more historically powerful. What we call incarnation (and in doing so we unhesitatingly think of Christian Platonism and its modern surrogate manifestations) is merely an episode within the eternal linguistic and spiritual resplendence (*Aufleuchten*) of the *physis,* which has been going on forever.

Presumably, in the dawn of advanced culture, the impression must have occurred that there existed an autonomous sphere of ideas, values, deities, and commandments, which would have to descend into the physical world in order to accomplish its spritualizing work—its *opus operandum*—within it. "And the word became flesh and dwelt among us": this *hymnus* of Christian Platonism is at the same time the motto of advanced cultures that *eo ipso* represent programs for moralizing, spiritualization, education, and excarnation. Therefore, advanced cultures must also always constantly appear as cultures that represent the inner war waged by a mobilizing and conquering intellect against a languid and suffering flesh. There is at work within them, in addition to the external violence of war and domination—perhaps as the strongest characteristic—the incarnate violence of the word, which entered the body in order to elevate its sorrow, desire, indolence, and self-will into a radiant "function."

A more patient analysis, however, will reveal that this is a false description— or at least an inadequate one, which mistakes only half of the phenomenon for the whole. For speech itself is always older than the *logos* of advanced culture; from the very beginning, bodies have spoken their "moods," their "taste," and their excitation, before an empowering word could dictate to them what they were to say or incarnate. Since human existence depends on sharing (*Teilen*) and communicating (*Mitteilen*) because of older somatic fundamentals, no real foundation exists for a *logos* that would prefer to cut itself away from its physical foundation in order to tyranically monopolize it. *Logos* is merely the parasite of an older linguistic predilection that responds only secondarily and in a highly cultured way to the violence and catastrophic conditions of the civilizing process; *logos* always creeps upward along the unendurability of a universal condition within which life appears as something that must be overcome, and, if not as this, then at least as something that is meant to be observed from above: thus the old affinity between spiritualization and mortification, both of which are symptoms of the logopathology (*Logopathie*) of advanced culture. But even the excesses of logofication are only the bifurcations of the primary communicativity of the living, which still has the capacity to recognize itself in its abuses.

Does Nietzsche's own work corroborate these observations? I believe he is one of the few thinkers to fulfill, in an exemplary manner and from a modern perspective, the tendency to become language, which is inherent in *physis*. He was a genius of correspondences; he survived the experience of universal arrival and concession, of excitation and resonance, of phenomenon and correspondence, in a overwhelming way. Looking back on the ecstasies he experienced during the writing of *Zarathustra,* he found astonishing formulations for the surplus of words that were available for expressing the factual matter of life:

> Here all things come caressingly to your speech and flatter you, for they want to ride on your back. . . . all being wants to become word here,

all that is in the process of becoming wants to learn to speak from you. (*KSA*, 6, p. 340)

Shortly before the beginning of the twentieth century—which is *the* linguistic century—a linguistic phenomenon occurred that no linguist could ever have imagined. How did Nietzsche transcribe it?

> With the very least residue of superstition within oneself, one could hardly know how to rid oneself of the idea that one is mere incarnation, merely a mouthpiece, merely a medium for powerful forces. (*KSA*, 6, p. 339)

One would have to extinguish even the final remainders of superstition in order to find one's way back through the metaphysical fog to the truth of what was most evident: the fact that here no higher meaning was being incarnated—rather, a *physis* was expressing itself to the limits of overexposure (*Verstrahlung*). In this borderline area, there is no active difference between expression in and of itself and expressing *something*. At the edges of language, the difference between existence and speech is extinguished in the unavoidable fulfillment of absolute expression. That a maximum of physical well-being was added to these preconditions indicates that Nietzsche could find the rhythm of a successful life only if he freed himself from the compulsion to incarnate, so as to be able to yield to expression *before* language:

> My muscular ease was always greatest whenever my creative powers were most active. The *body* is enraptured; we can leave the "soul" out of our discussion. (*KSA*, 6, p. 341)

Nevertheless, his idea of being a medium, of performing the function of a mouthpiece, is not merely a superstitious mistake. It is tantamount to the insight that, in advanced culture's bathing of the body with the radiation of language, a compulsion and seduction are at work that do not stem from the speaker himself, and which cause him to say things that he does not say of his own accord (*von sich aus*) in the most precise sense. The spoken language is, indeed, not my own, or at least not *entirely* my own; it is always the others who have made me speak and listen to a language. Real speaking always occurs only in relation to hearing—above all, to having been heard. These inspired verbal emotions (*Wortergriffenheiten*) result in the effect, as strange as it is understandable, that, through the speaker, the Other only now, as it were, begins to speak. We call these strange episodes of linguistic life "inspiration," in which the designations and inscriptions that *logos* has left behind within the individual begin to resound against the instrument of the body as if they were our own property. Within the context of aesthetic inspiration we observe how *physis* embraces, surpasses, dances around and appeases the *logos;* in such moments the impression suggests itself that a sort of music is the mother tongue tongue of life. (According to Friedrich Hebbel, "Prior to becoming human, we heard music.") Within such inspired speech, the maternal and paternal tongues resound through the mouthpiece of the child of this world. The forebears make use of this child as a sign (*Zeichen*) for the expressions that could not be expressed during their existence. It is the dumb desire to be one of the Others that inscribes the hyperplastic linguistic body of the child so that this body might express what it is incapable of expressing itself. "Everything that is in the process of becoming wants to learn to speak from you." In the very name used to designate the child (*infans*, "the one who does not speak"), a process that aims toward making it a being who does speak comes into play, a process that is identical to the last detail to that of incarnation. Without the incarnation of *logos*, the subject would not enter into advanced culture, and without violation, there would be no incarnation of *logos*. Violation and *logos* belong together because only through violation can the speaker be compelled to say things that are directed against the vital interests of the *infans*. To speak in accordance with a *logos* means to speak the language of those who can make use of me only as someone who is obedient and deadened; *logos* is the epitome of values and words in the name of which we take part in partial and total self-mortification.

But how could we define a culture that would be successful in positive terms? Must culture inevitably be reduced to a subtle program of self-mortification and self-violation? By no means, for even if culture always has violence as part of its inheritance, it is free to release alert participants in the civilizing process from violation into creative play, the conscious endurance of what is painful, and humoristic subversion to the highest purposes. Every speaker who investigates the matter can attempt to bring the violence he has inherited to life in positive terms through partially obsequious, partially insurrectional analogies to its incarnational duties (*Inkarnationsaufträgen*), in order to express again what is its own after being released from the cultural curriculum that has been demanded by *logos*. To express what is its own, however, means being able, in a cheerful way, to say *nothing* more; it means getting behind the *logos* and reuniting with the older communicativity of the living. Thus, a risk-laden drama is plotted out within every psyche in advanced culture — the wrestling match between the reason of the body and the madness of its incarnations. Within advanced culture, *every* subject is pregnant with madness.[11]

In Nietzsche, a drama of madness results whenever Dionysus meets Diogenes. In the preceding discussion we have played with the question of which post-Zarathustrian mask would remain available to this thinker after he played himself out in the impossible role of the nonreligious originator to the very limits of what is humanly possible. Now it becomes clear that this question has been incorrectly phrased: a subsequent mask would have been inconceivable on the stage upon which the drama has been carried out up to this point. Only the countenances that belong to the speaker's program for incarnation can appear upon this stage. After this, only one decision remains: whether to demolish the stage, an act that is tantamount to the suspension of the attempt at incarnation; or to escape into the madness of a final embodiment, the fatal process of becoming a god.

Whenever Dionysus encounters Diogenes, this decision comes into play. It is the final performance of civilization—performed within the fragile body of an individual upon whom is thrust what he "was never permitted to want," the collision of Apollo and Dionysus, of *logos* and *physis,* of metaphysics and "kynical" wisdom. Here Diogenes stands for the playful body of an individual who would have saved his irresponsible sovereign expressiveness in that he suffuses all missions with irony—which results in his "language" sticking out its tongue at *logos*. If he stops to think properly, he does not have such terribly important things to say: he makes use of all languages to show how one is ultimately unable to say anything with them. Thus, *Sokrates mainomenos* and the music-making Socrates are ultimately one and the same. On the other hand, Nietzsche's Dionysus represents the phantasm of a body that wants to incarnate a divine *logos,* a body that is now only an instrument and speaks worlds, very nearly breaking the chains of individuation and the final indolence of the flesh so that it can unite the painful celebration of birth with that of life in a delirium of prophecy.

For an empirical individual, however, this incarnation of Dionysus is the unendurable pure and simple—identical to the manifestations of the unendurable, away from which all paths of culture lead toward what is endurable. No one, without having been prepared by something that is beyond the imaginable, can endure the shock effects of Dionysian radiation, and almost no one survives being immersed in what is unimaginable and irreparable.[12]

Nietzsche's metaphysical thesis on art provides the most impressive explanation for this: the compulsion toward art permeates existence at all levels. The unendurable must redeem itself into what can be endured; the irreparable must allow itself to be replaced; the unimaginable must allow itself to be represented; the irresponsible must accept responsibility for itself; what is immediately incommunicable must be communicated, and the indivisible must be broken up—so that it can endure itself. The *presence* must be brought back into the representation, because pure presence—apart from the unavailable exception of the mystical—is synonymous with the unendurable for human beings within the status quo.

This is where Diogenes makes his appearance—the crazy man who announces the deaths of god, *logos,* the empowered word, morality. He is the Dionysian savior from what is all too Dionysian. Because he has made it his business to experience the extremes, he has alerted himself to the possibility of adventuring in the intermediate sites. Held up before the backdrop of the Dionysian, banality begins to shine abysmally enough, and wherever this shining appears to be most life-enhancing, there sits Diogenes in his sunlight, lazy and deep, wary and happy, the personified denial of explosion, the illuminated prophylaxis against deadly radiation, the protector of the everyday, and the thinker of a Dionysian endurability. Diogenes warns the Dionysian philosopher against being ensnared in the trap of incarnation; he reminds him that there is no *logos* that would have authorized us to embody Dionysus—the ingenious corporeality of life itself already *is* Dionysus, and every duplication of this primary corporeality through the embodiment of an imaginary Dionysus could only lead to madness. Diogenes helps the Dionysian thinker to resist embodying ''god'' directly and being destroyed by the horror of the extraordinary. He protects him from burning too quickly. Thus, Diogenes to a certain extent incarnates the nonincarnation: he demonstrates his contented state of having nothing to say, and lives an existence that playfully withdraws from all duty. He practices, with the greatest presence of mind, the art of winning away from the empowered word a meaning that was intended by the powers themselves; he is the master of the art of subversion through humor. Diogenes opposes the pseudo-Platonic (as well as spiritual-Christian and modern-moralistic) hysteria of incarnation to the body's a priori attitude of ''Leave me in peace,'' which in itself already speaks enough.

The question as to the composition of Nietzsche's mask is, at base, a question as to the possibility of bringing the moralistic theater of incarnation of European metaphysics to an end. According to Nietzsche's response to this question, everything that has played a part in the fate of this thinker, even if only remotely, is remembered as horrible—horrible because, among other things, no one who has glanced even briefly behind the curtain of Western rationality can still pretend that Nietzsche's descent into madness was a private affair. This descent was, on the contrary, the individual recapitulation of an entire civilization, an exemplary sacrifice that, next to the death of Socrates and the slaughter of Jesus, represents a third unforgettable statement on the relationship between the empowered word and the expression of life within Western culture. ''Not only the reason of millennia, but their madness too, breaks out in us. It is dangerous to be an heir'' (*Thus Spoke Zarathustra,* ''On the Gift-Giving Virtue'').[13]

In his Dionysian farewell performance, Nietzsche sought reasons with which he could, in spite of everything, affirm his tormented life—this incarnation of the impossible. What would he not have given for the chance to breathe a sigh of relief within the context of an everyday existence that would have allowed him to let the matter of god *auf sich* rest and no longer violate his body, the miserable carriage horse.[14] He longed, because of the confusion of his compulsion toward incarnation, for an ultimate nakedness and simplicity: it is not least of all because of this that the word ''cynicism'' so frequently haunts the writings of his last conscious years.[15] Perhaps, then, even a professorship in Basel would have been good for something, as a form of being, and the naked existence of a god would not have been as trying and compromising.[16] He would have had no more cultural gold in his body, which would have had to be exchanged for acknowledgment as a royal child and given away because of the collapse of the treasury.[17] He would have done something that was his own—he could have given culture its due, taken a fragment of unavoidable *logos* upon himself, and at the same time fulfilled his task of incarnation honestly and artfully. Only then would he have been able to release himself to what he was: not a word become flesh, which irritated the dry masculine body with hopeless pregnancies, not a hysterical idea that dragged the body behind it as a melancholy casualty—but a silent, spiritually rich, playful *physis,* a concrete individuality beyond missions and resignations.

A Parmenideic moment awaits an individual such as this who has returned from the battlefields of the drama of individuation to that which can be endured. If the partiality of circumstances opposes it, it may experience being as a successful and unsurpassable recognizability. It encounters the great moments in which existence, corporeality, and knowledge are conceived of as a unified whole. From this point forward, everything is comedy—the war is over, research has come to an end. In every second of its existence the world would be acknowledged as being enough. Now a thought that leaves no shadow blossoms forth without need for transcendent worlds, without reduction, without imputation, supported only by a perception that is free from the weight (*Lidschlag*) of the researching ego, without interference and without the necessity of indulgence, immaculately looking the obvious in the eye. It is the midday of being, the calm lull of obligation (*Sollen*). The weight of the world has been lifted; there is incorrigibility wherever we look. Dionysus is philosophizing.

Chapter 5
Pain and Justice

There are many good inventions on earth, some useful, some
pleasing: for their sake, the earth is to be loved.
                                    Thus Spoke Zarathustra,
                                    "On Old and New Tablets"

So, would a raving individualism be Nietzsche's last word? Did he leave behind
for us nothing but the incentive for the production of ecstatic freethinkers in their
reckless physicality, their amoral intensity, and their suspicious second innocence?

We might ask: Where is the social, Herr Nietzsche? Are your ecstasies still
grounded on the constitution? Doesn't your commonplace conceal the landmines
of anarchy? What do you have to say about the problems of the present—or will
you limit yourself to a reference to the discrepancy between isolated knowledge
and collective banter? Is all that we can expect of you a subjectivity without a
subject, which, if thought out further as a general principle, cannot produce anything more than a postmodern colloquium, entitled: "The Autumn Salon of Van-
ities, upon Which Intensities Collapse into Each Other, in a Manner That is Guar-
anteed to Be Meaning-Free and Polylogical"? Only bodies remaining, without
worlds? Only actors remaining, with no *engagement?* Only adventurers, with no
retirement insurance? Only projects of antiquity without the realism of late capitalism? Only the new vehemence without diplomacy and the social state? Do
you intend to invite us into chaos with your young conservative romanticism of
conflict and your Dionysian prowess in the art of breaking barriers? Don't your
cult of the moment and your worship of the exception bring the sociopolitical
premises of democracy to ruin, that is, the capacities to engage oneself commu-
nicably, to engage in long-term thinking, and to feel within the context of the
institution? Isn't there inherent within every individualistic agitation a playing
with fire, an impulse toward the relaxation of restraint, which encourages bru-

tality and intimidates caution, which defends a loss of control and robs the breath of responsibility? Isn't any emphasis of the singular at the same time a pillaging of the general, which thus contributes to an increase in tension between narcissism and the *Grundgesetz?*[1] You will become a danger to political culture, Herr Nietzsche, if you don't cease seducing those who are most sensitive into political resignation—not to mention those hardened types who borrow risqué doctrines from your writings so that they can carry out their brutality with a clear conscience. Which brand of politics was it, then, that thought it had found in your energetic romanticism a permit to start swinging? Do we have to make it any clearer?

What these questions allude to, assuming a minimal recall of political ideas, is clear enough. Their bluntness, however, stems from perceptions that are themselves imprecise: it stems from a definition of the world that is fundamentally false and that disintegrates into radical ambiguities as soon as this definition has been discredited. It presumes that, in a normal society, it is simply a matter of bringing together individuals who have grown up exhibiting an average sense of good will for the purpose of solving their common problems cooperatively. Whoever withdraws from this kind of cooperation because he wants something different falls under suspicion of being someone who is running away from reality—or some other type of irresponsible subject—who conceals his blindness for the social behind therapeutic and private ideologies of retreat, and who, in the worst cases, makes excuses for himself with Nietzsche's formulation of the aesthetic exoneration of life.

This opinion, which probably considers itself the healthy one, disintegrates under the first alert gaze into fragments, each of which is counterfeit—beginning with the pseudo-ontological concept of normality, moving on to the trivially moralistic postulate of goodwill, and continuing all the way to the self-dominating, inflated, vulgar-ontological block that, in the form of the bipartite illusion of the individual here and society there, stands in the way of any deeper understanding, and ultimately is summarized in the vulgar-political compulsive idea of the "common purpose." Only "common values" are lacking here as ontological catchalls. One cannot, of course, permit the use of the term "deeper understanding" with its educated-bourgeois *Gemütlichkeit*; he who moves on from the word to the matter itself (*Sache*) is pulled into a dramatic phenomenon in whose wake the vulgar-ontological block to a Dionysian understanding melts away. It is little wonder, then, that critical identities rebel against an understanding of this kind as they would against something that mortally endangered the population. Because "truth" indicates something terrible for the subjects of the status quo, it is only natural that they would defend themselves from behind their block against the enlightening phenomenon, the drama; they react critically because they really do *not* want to find what they purport to be seeking.

This much can be made plausible without any great effort: for the person who experiences existence as a drama that takes place above the Dionysian foundation of pain and pleasure (and who is the alert individual who would not approach such an experience occasionally?), moral and social facts must appear as subordinate quantities, however much they try to force themselves into the discourses of the institution as realities of the first order. Nietzsche's theory of truth explains to us in the most impressive terms that what calls itself reality within the context of institutional discourse can be nothing other than a reality in place of a reality, an Apollonian explanation, ritualization, and institutionalization of the foundation of the world (*Weltgrundes*) in accordance with the criteria of endurability and predictability. But in the alert individual, this self-representation can never become exclusive: the individual is always standing at the crossroads; he is always alive only to the extent that he is a meeting point between the Dionysian and the Apollonian, i.e., that he occupies the position wherein reality, in its incapacity to be represented, encounters the institutional "reality in the place of reality" that can be verbalized.

It could therefore be that individuals who are alert to Dionysus are most decidedly *not* trying to dodge reality, but are rather the only ones who are able to survive in the vicinity of pain and pleasure—with all the ramifications of this survival for a metabolic exchange (*Stoffwechsel*) between the individual and nature, life and society, while, conversely, the completely politicized, completely socialized, and thoroughly moralized subjects would be the very ones who were most successful in their organized flight from the terrible truth. It is conceivable that no one is more translucent, authentic, more incorporated, or more life-enhancing in their involvement in what is real than these Dionysian individuals— these types who are unclassifiable, oversensitive, apolitical, or parapolitical. Perhaps it is they who engage themselves in an ecology of pain and pleasure that precedes any of the usual politics. Perhaps they are the real protopoliticians, as opposed to those who have specialized in "politics" with a capital *P* and those who, in the style of traditional activists, endlessly force their game as the administrators of abuses and as the agents of a shifting of suffering onto others.

Here a crack blatantly forms in the concept of the political itself. It will be necessary to supplement an everyday concept of the political—as the plane of combative and discursive interests along with their discourses, weapons, and institutions—with a darker, nighttime concept of the political that casts its gaze on the hidden ecology of universal pain. While politics, according to its everyday conceptualization, belongs to the Apollonian world of visibility and unfolds before our eyes as a reality in place of a reality, the dark side of the political falls on the side of the Dionysian—the nonconcrete energetic of a prototypical foundation of pain and pleasure, which is a prerequisite to all everyday political action and reaction. Within this dark conceptualization, the most sensitive problematic of modernity is announced; we are inquiring into the relationship between modern-day constructions of what is socially endurable, on the one hand, and the unendurable proliferation of suffering brought about by precisely such constructions of what can be endured, on the other. With this sort of dark inquiry, only one thing is obvious: wherever thought of this kind takes place, the logic of politology (*Politologien*) from Machiavelli to Marx and from Hobbes to Ho Chi Minh has already been superseded by a Dionysian politology of passions.

This is dangerous thought—how else could it be defined? Is it the usual anarchic-romantic flirtation with the abyss, the well-known playing with fire, which leads to the potential for conflict within the masses, a literary sharpening of an asocial explosive that every socialized subject carries within him? These are imputations with which any thinking in this area will have to reckon. I do believe, however, that one of the fundamental impulses of modernity is continued through such questions. In its best moments, enlightenment was always a phenomenon in the spirit of a Dionysian politology. Authentic modernity accomplished an immeasurable departure from the feudal ontology of *misere,* which was grounded in the fact that the very fewest had permitted the greatest number to suffer—a departure in which liberalism, Marxism, anarchism, social democracy, and political Catholicism by and large have come to terms with each other. The modern pain-ecological consensus—that the great majority will not allow themselves to be made to suffer by the minority forever—is the smallest common denominator for all the positions available within the fissured landscapes of modernity. Modernization has been accomplished for the most part as a mass entrance on the part of suffering subjects into what has been rendered newly endurable—into alleviations, authorizations, and enrichments that, when measured against traditional standards, were so overpowering that one was for a long time at a loss even to pose the question as to the ecology of their unburdening effects.[2]

This inability to pose the question has been coming to an end within the context of a dramatic awakening that has taken place over the last several decades. With spectacular speed, the feeling has spread that modernity cannot be satisfied with an exoneration of life from the ethos of technical improvement, political participation, and economic enrichment, but that it also longs for a Dionysian exoneration of life in the sense of an algodicy[3]—this feeling is the epochal basis for Nietzsche's new currency. As we see, the religious question has survived the end of religions. It now appears, insofar as it is articulated at the heights of modernity, as the question of the possibility of an aesthetic exoneration of life.

Of course, this question ultimately ties in with doubts as to the value and longevity of any improvements and the possibility of realizing general participation, doubts that have taken on epidemic proportions; in addition to this, these questions have their foundation in a skepticism vis-à-vis the moralism of sociopolitical modernity that is rapidly becoming radicalized. This skepticism allows us to ask whether, in the moralism of the Enlightenment, the legitimate voice of wounded life that is demanding its restitution can really be heard, or whether the syndrome of moralizing social activism has not long since unwillingly become part and parcel of the tendencies that, from behind the pretext of further improvement and humanitarian progress, lead to an unprecedented proliferation of suffering.

In a situation such as this, what could be more suggestive than Nietzsche's doctrine of the aesthetic exoneration of life? Whoever takes the aesthetic into consideration as an exonerating force has broken through the spell of the moralistic concept of exculpation that clings to the Protestant wing of modernity in particular and has burdened us with libraries full of dyspeptic moral discourses. With its assertions in this respect, Nietzsche's *Birth of Tragedy* has won a philosophical breadth that exceeds everything debated prior to it. For, with a recklessness that is still astonishing today, Nietzsche cut through the moral knots of modernity. He naturalistically reversed the relationship between morality and life: instead of finding fault with life from the perspective of an eternally dissatisfied morality, he began by observing morality from the perspective of an eternally unimprovable life. This reversal provides the "suggestive statement" that "the existence of the world can be justified only as an aesthetic phenomenon" with its penetrating power—and explains why it is unacceptable for those who even today maintain the primacy of the moral.

On the question of pain, the intellectuals are divided. Actually, we are dealing with two diametrically opposed definitions of what constitutes the pain of life. The moral-political definition, which—unjustly and for too long—has wanted to be perceived as the only legitimate voice of enlightenment, recognizes in almost all pain a variation of injustice and derives from it a program for its redress that expands into sociopolitical—indeed, historical-philosophical—perspectives. Moralistic-theoretical modernity wants to respond to the question of algodicy with a progressive universal analgesic in which pain can only find acknowledgment of its own potential abolition as an ontological motif. That this is an uncontemptible view that becomes apparent as reasonable within an intermediate area does not require confirmation: a great majority of therapeutic action has been grounded on its plausibility. He who has suffered and found release knows how to evaluate its truth content. Was it not also Nietzsche who most clearly expressed what grief had to say about itself? Begone!

Accordingly, Nietzsche's algodicy stands in direct opposition to a program of moral abrogation. In a manner that is completely antiquated, it pits our memory of the ethos of the affirmative resistance against the modern idea of an abolishing negation. Because it conceives of life, in a radically immanent fashion, as the play acted out upon the foundation of pleasure and pain that cannot be overcome, it negates any metaphysics of redemption—including its modern manifestations in programs for the elimination of pain and therapy. Would this imply that Nietzsche was a stoic in the wrong century? Or does an irredeemable Christ want to throw the promises of the Christian age, with neoclassical gestures, onto the wreckage?

> Dionysus versus "the crucified"—there you have the opposition. It is not a difference with respect to martyrdom—it has a different meaning. Life itself, its eternal fertility and return, requires agony, destruction, the will to annihilation. . . . On the other hand, suffering, "the crucified one as the innocent," functions as an objection to this life, as a formula for condemning it. One guesses: the problem is that of the meaning of suffering, whether this be a Christian meaning, or a tragic meaning. . . . In the former case, it is meant to be the path to a divine being; in the latter, being is considered divine enough to vindicate a monstrous amount of suffering. The tragic human being still affirms the harshest suffering. . . . The Christian will negate even the happiest destiny on earth; the god on the cross is a curse upon life, a cue to redeem oneself from it; the Dionysus who has been cut to pieces is a promise of life: it is eternally reborn and brought back from destruction. (*Werke*, 15, p. 490)

Nietzsche's doctrine of the aesthetic exoneration of life reveals itself as the opposite of a cynical aestheticism: it is grounded in an algodicy that attempts to draw pain into the immanence of a life that no longer requires redemption as an element of the Dionysian passion. Within the Dionysian passion, which forms the basis for every alert life, there occurs, paradoxically, that which we have characterized as the endurance of the unendurable. But this endurance is not without its digressions; rather, it has two indispensable assistants in the form of intoxication and the dream—these oldest of drugs for elevating the psyche. They contribute to the formation of those intermediate worlds and realms of endurability that we need to keep ourselves from perishing of immediacy.

Here the thesis that *The Birth of Tragedy* must be read as Apollonian in its dramaturgical effect again becomes important. The book had shown how Dionysian passion has been instructed by means of an Apollonian translation into something that can be looked at, imagined, and endured. In this book, Nietzsche professes culture, the compulsion to symbolize, representation. That this profession has a double base was made just as clear—for if culture then wanted to belong in general to the world of illusion, it would be a matter of an illusion that does not permit anyone to look through it because it is the true lie of life itself. Accordingly, culture would be the fiction that we ourselves *are;* we exist as self-inventions of the living being that has been brought forth from the unendurability of the immediate Dionysian passion into a state of endurability and mediation. Life itself owes its spontaneous elevation to culture to a dialectic of what can be endured and what is unendurable, a dialectic from which the process of self-representation has sprung. From this, an ethics can be conceptualized from Nietzsche's basic assertions that is commensurate with the universal experience of modernity—an ethics of necessary illusion, of what is endurable, of intermediate worlds; an ethics of the ecology of pleasure and pain; an ethics of ingenuous life. The concept of illusion in Nietzsche possesses a power that bridges the contradiction between the ethical and the aesthetic—and, indeed, between the therapeutic and the political.

Under Nietzsche's gaze, the world of moral and political institutions is presented as a sphere of essential illusion, as a form of self-composition of collective life, which—in order to endure itself—must symbolize itself, ritualize itself, and subordinate itself to values. These suppositions form the Apollonian backbone of culture. One could (vis-à-vis his book on tragedy) compare them to what was initially said about Nietzsche's construction of the tragic stage: they would be like these Apollonian support mechanisms, through whose efficiency a culturally endurable arrival of the Dionysian would become possible for the first time. But the normative sphere of law, mores, conventions, and institutions receives its legitimation from life's compulsion toward art, *not* from the autonomy of a universal law of morals (*Sitten*). However, in order to remain valid, moral law must appear in the guise of autonomy and universality. There will be no Apollonian ethics without Dionysian foundation, but there can also be no Dionysian ethics without Apollonian fictions of autonomy. This means that, after Nietzsche, there can no longer be a theory of culture that is not informed by fundamental ironies. Nietzsche did indeed shift moral and cultural-critical thought onto the track of naturalism, but he also broke open naturalism aesthetically and illusionistically; he localized this compositional, inventive, lying phenomenon within the phenomenon of life itself. Thus we see through everything that has been culturally imposed to its natural basis; this basis is at the same time, however, what ascends to the cultural and is composed into value systems. Thus human consciousness is placed ontologically in an ironic site, one from which the pretending animal is condemned to see through his own fictions. His awakening to this irony is at the same time an awakening to philosophy—it is not an irony that could lead to detachment nor an understanding that would provide distance. At this site, the mechanism for maintaining distance from life through knowledge breaks down. But one must play with that from which one is unable to distance oneself.

Nietzsche's algodicy therefore conceals the beginnings of a philosophical ethics—an ethics that clearly rests on a foundation of tragic irony. Because the moral illusion belongs to the self-composition of life, a naturalistic self-awareness is also not permitted to want to return to moral compositions. They belong irrevocably to the cybernetics of social beings. The Apollonian, conceived of cybernetically, signifies nothing other than the necessity of imprinting upon the amorphous compulsion of Dionysian forces and the chaotic multiplicity of the individual a controlling form, which is ruled by the law of "moderation," individuality, self-limitation, and rationality. The concept of "justice" is a true dream of humanity, born out of the unendurability of unjust conditions: it belongs to the self-regulation of life in the "intermediate worlds" of endurable homeostases. It is a component of the comprehensive compositions of self that we refer to as "cultures." But because everything just and all morality are to be understood as controlling forces in the cybernetics of the unendurable, the ironic shadow cast by the postulate of the autonomy and universality of justice will never again be skipped over. Where values are, there ironies shall be.[4] The slick Apollonian belief in values and their autonomy cannot be reproduced in modernity.

If ethics is cybernetics, we can understand why it pursues no objectives but, rather, processes breakdowns. It is a typically modern error to believe that ethics might change the world, to guarantee the Apollonian natural right to an endurable life. Nietzsche has classically formulated the regulative character of the ethical-Apollonian in that he advances the claim that only as much of the Dionysian foundation of pleasure and pain should be permitted to surface in an individual as "can be again subdued by the Apollonian force of transfiguration." Is it possible to conceive of a more sublime acknowledgment of culture?

Here the concept of righteousness appears with an unusual significance. For Nietzsche states further on in the same discussion:

> Thus these two art drives must unfold their powers in a strict
> proportion, according to the law of eternal justice. (*BT*, p. 143)

Justice now becomes the heading for a homeostatic ethics, the necessity of which is based on the self-regulation of living processes. Nietzsche formulates this paradoxically enough: "All that exists is just and unjust and equally justified in both" (*BT*, p. 72). He who expresses himself in this way does not sit at his desk and draw up the plans for better worlds; he does not analytically pull to pieces the moral vocabulary of his nation and, on the basis of this accomplishment, take himself for a philosopher. He who speaks in this way has, through experimentation on his own body, thrust forward into the tissue of reality and cast his gaze into the ecology of suffering life.

Of course, this has for some time not been a matter of what is dealt with in formal ethics or doctrines of material value. Behind the altercations between good and evil and the contest of values for cultural or political priority there arises—defiant and threatening—the central philosophical massif of modernity: the question of understanding subjectivity as such. With the introduction of a cybernetic concept of justice, something decisive has clearly taken place—something that is heavy with implications and that must remain plainly incomprehensible and unacceptable to those who have inscribed upon their flags the illusion of the moral autonomy of the subject and the superstition of free will. The moral subject—whether it is called "individual," "citizen," "entity with legal rights," "human being," or whatever—has with this turn of events already been released from its fictional central position in the moral cosmos. It has become "decentered" into a great force within the play of subjecivté forces. Here the question of whether a surrender or release of the subject has taken place must remain unanswered; a decision on this could not be made readily in any case. It is not unthinkable that only a decentering of the subject, which bids a respectful adieu to the fiction of autonomy, could lead to a legitimate constitution of subjectivity—beyond ego and will. What seems at first a bitter expulsion from the center could be viewed on second glance as an adventurous enrichment—if it is correct that, in becoming conscious of having been decentered, the subject is anyway only giving up what it never possessed—its autonomy—and is gaining what it would have to lose to the illusion of autonomy: the play of its body and its dialogic-ecstatic status. Whereas the centered subject is the effect of a grammatical system that harasses to death the living consciousness between "Thou shalt" and "I want," the decentered subject would perhaps be the first to have the right to say in reference to itself: I am.

What is to be gained from these speculations? Assuming that they pointed in the direction of fruitful insights, who would gain by learning to accept a cybernetic version of justice and seeing in it a radical, constructive, selective force that belongs to the constructive nature of vital self-composition? The significance of these speculations lies presumably only in their ramifications for the self-definition of the phenomenon of enlightenment. Because enlightenment represents a historic wager on the realization of a reasoning subjectivity, the subject of enlightenment is radically moved by a transformation of the concept of the subject from a moral-legal center of will to a cybernetic and medial phenomenon. This is no small matter. It is presumably an all-or-nothing situation being put into play within the context of philosophical thought. The subject of enlightenment could from this point forward no longer constitute itself as it had wanted to in accordance with the rules of Apollonian illusionism as an autonomous source of meaning, ethos, logic, and truth—but, instead, as something medial, cybernetic, eccentric, and Dionysian, as a site of sensibility within the ruling cycles of forces, as a point of alertness for the modulation of impersonal antagonisms, as a process of self-healing for primordial pain, and an instance of the self-composition of primordial pleasure—to speak poetically, as an eye through which Dionysus observes himself.[5]

Measured against such conceptions of medial subjectivity, the moral constructivism of the Enlightenment must appear naive. If, indeed, the vision of a universal dominion of morality is derived from this, this naïveté becomes a hysteria—a procreation of demons in the air, an impotent self-begetting of Apollonian illusion. In his critique of morality, Nietzsche presents us with a minimum of a second reflection, without which the Enlightenment for its part would remain only a natural illusion. A morality without morals is unthinkable, however, without an aesthetic relationship to the necessary illusion:

> If we could imagine dissonance become man—and what else is man?— this dissonance, to be able to live, would need a splendid illusion that would cover dissonance with a veil of beauty. (*BT*, p. 143)

The Apollonian veil is just as moral as it is aesthetic in nature and is woven in particular from the most magnificent of all self-disillusionments, which the Enlightenment had characterized as the moral autonomy of the subject. Thus man, according to his moral ecology, is a fragment of suffering, dreaming, building, and valuing nature that—in order to endure itself—needs the illusion of freedom from merely suffering naturalness.

These thoughts are anything but pleasant. They indicate that Nietzsche's doctrine of the aesthetic exoneration of life does not represent a program of frivolity. To a much greater extent, it is one of the most serious attempts—perhaps the only promising one—to think through the moral situation of modernity without being duped into the more complex swindle of a New Morality. The seriousness of this attempt is connected with the audacity of the attack against recent abstract subjectivism. There shines forth from Nietzsche's project the beginnings of a return to the physical foundation of justice—comparable to the return to the physical foundation of thought discussed in Chapter 4. In both cases, the truth is speaking as a truth from below, not as an idea in search of a body, but as an intelligent body that, out of respect, accelerates itself in the course of its composition of self toward language, toward the intellect, and toward justice in a manner that is stringently perspectival, "constructive," "eliminating," and "destructive".[6] However, the notion that knowledge does not fall from heaven, but instead opens itself to us through the dramatic revelation of previously concealed worldly realities, is *the* fundamental concept of authentic modernity—regardless of whether it speaks a scientific, "depth-psychological," Marxist labor-oriented, anthropological, or fundamentally ontological idiom. In the ciphers of physicality, a *Dionysian materialism* is announced, of which "dialectical" materialism is only a brutal caricature.

With these observations, we leave the realm within which we had been able to read *The Birth of Tragedy* as an aesthetic theory with cultural-philosophical sidelights. In my concluding remarks I will attempt to advance Nietzsche's model to a level at which his book on tragedy will take on a wide-range, "truth-historical" profile.

It actually seems to us as if Nietzsche, along with the major portion of his work, belonged within a history of the "enlanguaging" (*Versprachlichung*) and self-mobilization of *physis* that is incalculable but global in its implications—a phenomenon, therefore, for which the expression "Dionysian materialism" was used, an expression whose plausibility goes hand in hand with its unapproachability. And talk of materialism within modernity runs the risk of being complicit with the most brutal subjectivisms and the most cynical forms of objectifying thought. And yet, the materialist confession wanted, in accordance with its spirit, to reconcile with matter as the not-other of spirit; it strove to mediate the metaphysics that was unhappily hovering above the physical basis with it, and to call home the logical ghosts. Modern materialism, outlined in a quasi-maternally legitimate withdrawal of idealism, established itself almost universally as the form of thought for ultimate violation and the final seizure of power, and it seems to me that there belongs with it a belief that is more despairing than naive toward the historical potential and the power of self-control of modernity, in order to once again conjure up from beneath the unity of modernity in the spirit of a Dionysian materialism and a medial process of becoming universal.

Be that as it may, this thought always has the greater power, the more consequential structure, and the deeper universal capacity for containment vis-à-vis numerous retrogressive metamorphoses, enclosures, and degenerations. It is a thought that conceives of itself as materialist and Dionysian because it is permitted to believe in itself as a medium for a singularly phenomenal, dramatic universality. It knows that it has been incorporated into a planetary magnetism of physical universal candor (*Weltoffenheit*) that shows us that every delimitation of subjectivity that does not become superegotistical raving flows into trips around the world that parade before our eyes where our effective limits lie. Within these trips around the world on the part of a cosmonautical and a psychonautical reason that are both limitless and final at once, the freedoms of the modern era find their first fragile meaning. Cosmonautical reason concerns itself with the planets as the source and basis of a worldwide communion, world trade, world communication, and world ecology—and, when in crisis, world war. Psychonautical reason, on the other hand, queries the individual as to his capacity to endure the universal citizenship into which he was born. For this reason, I believe, the psychologies that have been developing continuously on European terrain for the last two hundred years are the essential component of authentic enlightenment; they are the symbolic vehicle of psychonautical reason, that is, any form of self-reflection that gives voice to our condition of being condemned to universality, even into the very depths of the subject. Within the phenomenon of Dionysian materialism, the individual psyche must be confronted with the advent of an increasingly violent and subtle contextualization of what constitutes the "world"; it must learn to liberate the unceasing unveiling of a world of worlds from its initial unendurability and recast it into something that can be endured. It must learn to accept into itself the impact of the much-too-much, which "arrives" from without, in order to correspond to the external opening of worlds through an increase in inner openness to the world—Dionysus is the deity who also protects the ecstasies of learning. The fundamental question for modern psychologies, which the Dionysians of an active materialism must render animate from the outside in, is the following: how can individuals who are imprinted by regionality, finiteness, and fear of death in any way endure being affiliated with a planetary fact? To formulate this in the language of Heidegger: how can finite being (*Dasein*) endure being thrown into an irrepressible universality?

Nothing is more complicated than an answer to this question. But what does this help? The arrival of the God to come is accomplished today in Dionysians of complexity. He who concerns himself with modernity as the period in which he exists will more than ever have to find his way back in complicated stories.

I recently made an attempt to untangle one of the complicated threads of modernity in a philosophical story. I wanted to show how the depth-psychological mediation of body and world had been made obligatory for modern individuals before the models of Nietzsche, Freud, and Jung existed. One has to reach back into the period of the French Revolution to observe the decisive moment at which the unconscious began to emerge.[7] The unconscious is the name for the sources at which the modern (i.e., postreligious) retrogressive metamorphoses of subjectivity lead back to that which preceded it. The body and the drama are the material foundations of this modern consciousness of retrogressive metamorphoses; we experience in them the way in which the narrowness of the subject breaks open when it resigns itself *nolens volens* to the universal context, of which it has long since unconsciously been a part and from which it will never be permitted to escape. Any inwardness is interwoven deeply and somatically into the magnetism of the universal.

It has been said that the three decisive revolutions of the nineteenth century were the politicization of the proletariat, the cultural seizing of language by women, and the discovery of the unconscious. Could it not be that the same phenomenon was at work in all these movements, which would only now be apostrophied as Dionysian or dramatic materialism? Is it not in each case a matter of the surfacing of amorous and plural truths that, thanks to the revolutionary exonerations of technical civilization, are able to develop a modern ecology of expression?

It is probably impossible properly to understand Nietzsche's idea of justice if one views his work and his person as separate from these movements of emergence. It would above all else be an unjust abbreviation to explain Nietzsche's impulse as representing only an oscillating balancing with the immoralistic derestraining tendencies of advanced capitalism that are produced in advance, whether this might also exhibit what belonged to the image of an active nihilism together with its "constructive," "excluding," "exterminating" determinations of value. One would be much more likely to do justice to Nietzsche if one could conceive of his work as a play in the twilight—the twilight of the idols of metaphysics and the collapse of idealisms. This would be appropriate to the emergent movement of the excluded physical and dramatic forces. After having been wounded, banished into the darkness, and forgotten, the bodies that have all too long been abused as incarnation machines press toward the light; they make use of modern exonerations, authorizations, and symbolic constructs to prepare for a new intervention by the lower elements—for a new presence of the 'basis," which cunningly and as a rule behaves as if it wanted something in particular and as if it were fighting for a place in the sun of subjectivities, while at bottom it is always only looking for a chance to once again become aesthetic and appear in the arena of absolute self-representation.

But whereas, among these basis movements, the proletarian and feminist movements are more easily caught by the traps of subjectivity of abstract individualism, the emergent movement of the unconscious—even in its ego-psychological reversal and its therapeutic alienation—remains the most promising manifestation of the three. The depth psychologies, which for two hundred years have increasingly left their mark on the physiognomy of intellectual Europe, are the characteristic impulse in the history here described as Dionysian-materialist. They conceal the most important reasoning potential of an enlightenment that is not only instrumental and strategic: only they are prepared to consider properly the reality of the drama under the conditions of modernity. Wherever they remain true to their authentic impulse, they reject the deliberate indolence of rationalism and decline to cooperate with the abstract individualism that is only the psychic-legal form in which the universal domination of a nature-exploiting theoretical-moralistic subject wants to prevail. The depth psychologies are, as it were, the thinking heart of the modern, which must beat during the epochal history of refusing light to the *physis* if all bodies are not to atrophy into intersubjectivized fighting machines and self-consciously cold legal entities. This heart thinks in the center of Dionysian passion—within the memory of the ecology of suffering, among which are included even the reason of exonerations and the construction of what is endurable. It is the living memorial that the history of the wounding of civilization has accumulated within itself, along with all of what must be consolidated of induration and obscuration in order to bring forth the dominant degree of intellectual armament and the armoring of the body.

Admittedly, this all sounds a trace too dark to satisfy the need for understanding, in case one anyway and of one's own accord does not know what could be meant. Is the author here making a game, following the example of the more recent French authors, of cultivating darkness as a genre of the beaux arts? Or is it plausible that the veil over these references to a depth-psychological drama of knowledge should not be understood as a malicious component of a literary nature but instead illuminated as a ways and means by which the "thing itself" is there for us? How could our thinking, if it questions the limitations of its performance, circumvent the insight that it cannot render everything transparent? With the acknowledgment that the rational world is situated before an "arational'' background and that transparency is able to unfold only before the massif of what is nontransparent, enlightenment can leave behind it the arena of an omnipotent illuminating infantilism and reach the level of a maturity that can criticize reason. What Merleau-Ponty has observed of the philosopher — that he carries with him a shadow that ''signifies more than the factual absence of potential light'' — can be applied on the whole to enlightenment.

What does this all mean? It is easier to say what if does not mean. It does not mean, for instance, that something like a depth-psychology-related enlightenment of society should be undertaken immediately; it does not mean that we should make something of the insight into the dramatic, dark structure of subjectivity, something like a psychotherapy in the spirit of the production of individuals who are simultaneously Dionysian and socially functional. It also does not mean that it is high time to shift over into a loving interaction after centuries of organized egoisms. These negations do not intend to posit anything against loving interaction, psychotherapy, or the spirit of enterprise. What is being negated — or at least interrupted and ceased in its impulse — is the indisputably false reflexes that direct our behavior toward enterprise, production, and transferal. These reflexes, which are all supported by the myths of praxis, precede modern procedures for problem solving and the ideologies of engagement.

No other phenomenon illustrates this more clearly than the dramatic centerpiece of modern reason, against which even the depth psychologies have been defined. For depth-psychological processes — to define them in Nietzsche's terms, these are the drama, tragedy, and phenomena — are, according to the type of their occurrence, precisely that into which no production process or business enterprise can reach. They are the ontological model for what, because of its own form of being, for us, cannot be achieved, induced, or produced in accordance with a method. They stand out — within the dominant rationalism of availability — as monuments to the unavailability of what is most real. This remains always something that happens or does not happen beyond the subjectivities that are in operation: passionate love, spontaneous memory, phenomenological insight, pure success, a happy synchronicity, a clarifying failure, timely separation, the bursting forth of primordial pain — all of this paraphrases an area in which the Will is not able to have its way. We cannot be silent about the fact that, in any case, even depth-psychological consciousness has almost no defense against its attempts to establish itself in the form of technical praxis and to accept therapeutocratic social activism.

Here the recollection of Nietzsche's theory of the drama can once again prove useful. For Nietzsche clearly realized at the beginning — long before he set out on the trail to power as the universal formula of nihilistic activism — that the sort of tragedy in which mere calculating subjects play themselves is no longer possible: the ''show'' of the individual is the end of theater (one is reminded here of Nietzsche's critique of Euripides). The overpowering drama unfurls wherever individuals are not actors on their own volition, but are rather conduits for a phenomenon that is older than their awareness of themselves. The authentic drama is consummated as a Dionysian passion of the *physis,* which phenomenologically reminds itself of its individuation, its "destiny," and its "future." Accordingly, drama is by its very nature psychodrama: psychodrama, however, is the unity of memory and phenomenon, of knowledge and destiny. Therefore, enlightenment commands an indissoluble relationship to drama—even though the modern organization of knowledge tends to reformulate all problems of enlightenment into questions pertaining to the power to dispose of information. Knowledge, however, is the phenomenon of all phenomena and the destiny of all destinies. It continually has the character of a psychonautical process that is spun out on the Ariadne's web of the terrible truth. We must remind ourselves that the search of the hero—the conqueror and patient of knowledge—begins as a flight from the terrible truth; it can become a discovery if it leads to the conscious acceptance of the truth that has occurred and is occurring. On its spiritual journey, the subject is a nondivine nonsufferer searching for a divine patience—which is only another way of expressing the Dionysian integrity of life within the unity of lust, pain, and knowledge. Thus Dionysian wisdom does not teach a release from suffering; it does not believe in an evasive movement that leads upward. To a much greater extent, it gives us an understanding that at least frees us from suffering on account of our suffering.

Would it then follow that a therapeutics that is tragic, in Nietzsche's sense, would be the guiding light for an enlightened enlightenment? Would it provide the model for that understanding that could not be compelled by any procedure or rendered controllable by any method? One would not have to hesitate for a moment to write down this observation if a profession of a dramatic therapeutics were not once again being misunderstood by the activistically tainted *Zeitgeist* as a declaration of a position with a view to practicality. Thus the second, more elevated, enlightenment must begin with a hesitancy: an enlightened hesitancy is the glimmer of meditation and of epic patience that has more to do with the psychonautical adventure than would be revealed at first glance. For psychoanalysis in the current sense of the term can occur only if the subject is set aside so that its history, its drama, can be told. The term "psychoanalysis" here of course refers not to the compromised Freudian undertaking but rather to the whole of psychonautics, that is, of depth-psychological enlightenment occurrences that, for approximately two hundred years, have concerned themselves with the postreligious absorption of the subject into the space between aesthetics, therapeutics, and Dionysian reflection. To attribute such a high place value to depth-psychological dramaturgy within the process of enlightenment is in no way intended to channel water toward the mills of therapeutic actionism. The psychonautical phenomena of modernity are not directed toward guidelines for action: their process is eventful enough in and of itself.

We have in any case few models before us as suggestive of the fact that it is not rational action but rather a rational willingness to allow things to happen that can become the prerequisite for knowledge and enlightenment. He who knows from experience what this formulation "means" will perhaps be able to judge what elements are at stake in such speculations on the relationship between doing and permitting. It is a matter of nothing less than a sensible division of reason between the poles of subject and process; this is what must be characterized as postmetaphysical learning processes. A therapeutic drama at the level of universal civilization, which would be carried out without anyone authorizing or ordering it, would be a learning process that could bring to an end the assault of active nihilism, with its assignments of value, constructive measures, establishment of levels, and eliminations. Heidegger probably indirectly had something of this sort in mind when he cited Hölderlin's "But wherever danger resides, there also grows salvation." A planetary therapeutics that would occur without having a new central subject positioned above it seems to be the only thing that could bring the race for the salvation of subjectivities to a halt on their own account. Any activity in this area—even if it were the kind of "trust-building measures" that seem to have come directly from the vocabulary of Mephistopheles—would have to prove themselves as mere continuation, and in the meantime even children have learned that the great abysses of the present are all located as they were before on the straight line of continuation. Whether the name of the therapeutics of checking—and here the term takes on a fatal ring—must be "catastrophe" under any circumstances is the question of our age, if it is expressed in thought. One must let the thousand lesser devils for whom this is no longer a question, but rather a hope, have their poor malevolent fun.

Our reading of Nietzsche's book on tragedy leads to a sort of guideline for Dionysian learning, a term for which one could also say "therapeutics," "psychonautics," or "psychodrama"—yes, even "politics," insofar as one understands the expression in accordance with the concept of night elucidated earlier. Dionysian learning intends the flaring of insight to the point of danger, to a knowledge at the razor's edge: it characterizes thought on that stage from which there is no running away, because it is reality itself. Life is the trap that is a stage, and the stage that is a trap.

It is precisely within Dionysian learning, however, that Apollonian safety measures are necessary. The dramatic impulses of the actors may not be translated directly from the aesthetic (realm) to the political; Walter Benjamin's warnings on this point are still valid today. They must first be subjected to an Apollonian intervention that regulates the political ecology of suffering. Under today's conditions, a political act would have to slip all too rapidly from impulsiveness into fascism.

Let me put it this way: during the plunge from the body of the mother into late capitalism, the pain of individuation accumulates for which late capitalism as such cannot be held responsible—however close this reflex may be and as numerous as the discourses may be that tell us, in the course of the instinctive search for the guilty party, where he can be found. To process this pain, which belongs not to the realm of social information but rather to the cycle of life, on a subpolitical level, a self-aware antipolitical therapeutics is required—not to depoliticize individuals, but to deneuroticize politics, to protect the political from psychodynamic movements and Dionysian short circuits.[8] By therapeutics I mean, of course, not only the operation of psychologizing subcultures, but all techniques, rites, and games that contribute to the pleasure/pain ecology of social life—all paths of conscious life and all lines of psychonautics. If mythological, poetic, shamanistic, and neoreligious lines now increasingly appear among these, this does not indicate—at least from a functional viewpoint—an insult to the modern by a new irrationalism, but instead speaks to a well-meaning release of politics from the suspicion that it could be immediately responsible for the self-compositions and the sufferings caused by individuation in individual lives.

Within the new multiplicity of psychonautics, a mature sense of the distribution of responsibilities is revealed. One's misery thus consists not so much in one's sufferings as in the inability to be responsible for them—one's inability to *want* to be responsible for them. The will to accept one's own responsibility— which is, as it were, the psychonautical variant of the *amor fati*—indicates neither narcissistic hubris nor fatalistic masochism, but rather the courage and the composure to accept one's own life in all its reality and potentiality. He who wants to be responsible for himself stops searching for guilty parties: he ceases to live theoretically and to constitute himself on missing origins and supposed causes. Through the drama, he himself becomes the hero of knowledge—the patient of truth. If enlightenment is carried out in this sense, it leads to a Dionysian autonomy: this is as far removed from the autonomy of the subject of idealistic modernity as the embodied existence is from the illusion of "overcoming" existence.

The Dionysian therapeutics that has been spreading from European soil into the planetary standard for two hundred years contains the most pointed challenge to the dominant forms of pseudoenlightenment, which is continually searching for causes and other "guilty parties" in order to finally establish itself, driven by the dream of becoming a subject or a god, as ideal successor in the place of the guilty. Who can wonder that, in the course of this pseudoenlightenment, the account books of suffering of humankind and nature are bulging to the point of catastrophe.

He who senses the ruinous element in this uncontrolled pseudoenlightenment will recognize that Nietzsche—in spite of his unpredictable deviations and his malevolent tones—does not preach a counterenlightenment; to a much greater degree he, like no one else among the greater figures of modernity, set about to understand the concept of enlightenment as adventurous thinking to the very limits of pain. Almost one hundred years after the onset of his illness, Nietzsche can finally be read as he deserves to be: as one of those who, because of a Dionysian consciousness, raise their voices against the universal conspiracy of active indolence so that they can report to us on the loneliness and the "heavy, heavy happiness" of the unloved animal who says "I." Even he, together with his hopeless hardness and his sad battle of separation, can be read as someone in whom the tender empire of the body wanted to learn to speak once again. With his pathos of integrity, his feeling for sound, and his intellectual passion, he is not so far from the "reciprocal cautions"—to take up Jürgen Habermas's beautiful formulation—with which those who were born later are able, with a little communicative luck, to give their existence a better turn. It remains futile to ask what would have become of Nietzsche if he had unraveled the thread of Ariadne that led to *her,* the mistress of the labyrinth. His stage was from the very beginning constructed as a labyrinth, from which there was no escape to another. In his dramatic coming out of himself before the eyes of everyone and no one, however, he burrowed through, turned around, pushed to the pinnacle, and brought to an end an entire system of values, an entire civilization, an entire era. Those who live after him have an easier time of it. He has warned them of the three unforgivable original sins of consciousness: idealism, moralism, and *ressentiment.*

But nothing in Nietzsche's writing can have as great a continuing effect as his own refutation of his theory of the will to power. His whole life contradicts it and testifies to a stimulating fragility that is turned toward us like the hardly disguised interior of the terrible truth. Wherever he is wounded, endangered, and ingenuous, it is there that he is still among us; wherever his icy abundance buries him alive, it is there that he anticipates the fate of all later individualisms. Wherever he walks with transparent optimism over abysses, it is there that he demonstrates what it means today to be contemporary. And wherever he affirms the course of the world that is crushing him to death so that he can thus create a space for his self-affirmation, it is there that he is a witness to the happiness of those who are without hope.

Notes

Notes

All citations from *The Birth of Tragedy* (*BT*) are taken from Walter Kaufmann's standard translation (*The Birth of Tragedy and the Case of Wagner,* translated and with commentary by Walter Kaufmann [New York: Vintage Press, 1967]). Wherever possible, quotations from other works by Nietzsche are taken from known translations, for which bibliographic information is included. Translated quotations that include only a reference to the German edition and are not cited in the notes are my own. — Trans.

1. Centauric Literature

1. Letter from Ritschl, translated and quoted by Walter Kaufmann in his introduction to *The Portable Nietzsche* (New York: Viking Press, 1954), pp. 7–8. Notes for all subsequent quotations from this volume will give the title of Nietzsche's text, *PN,* and pertinent page numbers.

2. "Homer's Contest," *PN,* p. 37.

3. Letter to Erwin Rohde, in *Nietzsche: A Self-Portrait from His Letters,* ed. and trans. Peter Fuss and Henry Shapiro (Cambridge, Mass.: Harvard University Press, 1971), p. 10.

2. The Philology of Existence, the Dramaturgy of Force

1. "Gradually, it has become clear to me what every great philosophy so far has been: namely, the personal confession of its author and a kind of involuntary and unconscious memoir." *Beyond Good and Evil,* trans. Walter Kaufmann (New York: Vintage Books, 1966), p. 13.

2. This is not a simple "violation of self," as the psychologizing subjectivism of a popular critical mode of thinking would have it. It is at best an active acceptance of a "thrownness" (*Geworfenheit*) into a state of "already-having-been-violated" (*Schon-vergewaltigt-Sein*). With this, something is being outlined that belongs characteristically to the psycho-ontologicial phenomenon of masculinity. A very stimulating work on this theme is Günter Schulte's "*Ich impfe euch mit dem Wahnsinn*": *Nietzsches Philosophie der verdrängten Weiblichkeit des Mannes* (Frankfurt/Paris: Qumran, 1982).

3. The following comment betrays the extent to which Nietzsche consciously dealt with the his-

torical-mythological parallelism between Wagnerian modernity and Dionysian antiquity: "For me, the phenomenon of Wagner viewed in the flesh initially negatively illustrated the fact that we have up to now not yet understood the Greek world and, vice versa, that it is therein that we will find the only analogies to our phenomenon of Wagner" (*Kritische Gesamtausgabe Werke*, ed. Giorgio Colli and Mazzino Montinari [Berlin: W. de Gruyter, 1967ff.], 9, p. 232. Hereafter cited as *Werke*.)

4. I combine this statement with a question mark behind Lyotard's thesis, in accordance with which the postmodern condition is characterized by a radical loss of belief in all historical "meta-narratives," i.e., all philosophies of history. But what if the philosophy of history possessed no — or at least no apparent — narrative form? Perhaps history is not an epic phenomenon, but rather a theatrical one, comparable not to the novel but to the *commedia dell'arte*, in which the plot is carried along from scene to scene thanks to the improvisational powers of an ensemble of actors. If this were true, the usual polemic against any sort of historical-philosophical tension would be reduced to the level of a battle with critical windmills.

5. Lou Andreas-Salome places — in my opinion, correctly — the impulse toward release from the self at the center of her psychological portrait of 1894, *Friedrich Nietzsche in seinen Werken*.

6. Manfred Frank, *Der kommende Gott: Vorlesungen über die Neue Mythologie* (Frankfurt: Suhrkamp, 1982).

7. Here I mean the languages/voices of a secular inwardness that was cultivated from the eighteenth through the twentieth century — the symbolic space that extends from *The Magic Flute* to *The Magic Mountain*.

8. A twofold cultural defense mechanism can be perceived in Nietzsche's Dionysian discourse. Specifically, the romantic aesthetic of genius and the psychology of an inner duality symbolically conceal an actual state of psychic disruption. In general, the establishment of the symbolic register regulates the real unchaining of Dionysian forces in a manner that is culturally acceptable. Only through this powerful symbolic guarding are the psychodynamic processes of emergence and release from inhibitions in their entirety possible, processes that characterize the modern psychologies. Since the eighteenth century, an enormous thrust toward the breaking down of barriers, toward loosening and unchaining, has been set in motion within the bourgeois revolution in expression — even under the protection of new, intensive, civilizing defense mechanisms — a thrust whose unfolding we currently discuss under the misleading rubric of postmodernism.

9. "The . . . votary of Dionysus is understood only by his peers. With what astonishment must the Apollonian Greek have beheld him! With an astonishment that was all the greater the more it was mingled with the shuddering suspicion that all this was actually not so very alien to him after all, in fact, that it was only his Apollonian consciousness which, like a veil, hid his Dionysian world from his vision" (*BT*, p. 67).

10. At the end of Chapter 4 I will make several observations on the incarnation/psychosis problematic in Nietzsche's Zarathustrian "endgame."

3. *Cave Canem;* or, Danger, Terrible Truth!

1. It seems at present inevitable that, when we turn away from the vocabulary of the old European metaphysics, we fall back on concepts whose awkwardly physicalistic or old-fashioned vitalistic undertones will elude no one. That will happen here *faute de mieux* as well — in the assumption that it might be possible to use old and *sensu stricto* unsuitable words in a new way. It comes down to thinking through a surplus of formal, structural, and information-related instances within the context of the old physicalistic concepts of energy, i.e., of now including what has traditionally belonged on the intellectual side of metaphysical dualism in a material, process-related and textual concept that is postmetaphysical.

2. Nietzsche, *Kritische Studienausgabe*, ed. Giorgio Colli and Mazzino Montinari (Berlin: W. de Gruyter, 1967ff.), 6, p. 323. Hereafter cited as *KSA*.

3. There are within the psyche processes that are blatantly analogous to those that are involved in the accumulation of capital—and not just in a metaphorical sense. Producing subjects have to a great extent been organized in the form of subjective capital or learning mental machinery; subjective capitalism is the psychic reality of intellectual subcultures. Perhaps this is the source of the desolate lack of solidarity perceived by those who try to communicate with the intellectual public in a language that remains unwieldly in the face of the compulsions toward accumulation and self-armament characteristic of combative and self-exploitive intellects.

4. This is true at least for the public, didactic, and rhetorical aspect of his reflection. In his intimate observations, however, Nietzsche saw through the "will to power" as the manifestation of an esoteric comedy of subjectivity.

5. Hans Ebeling offers a reflection on occasional motives in a weakened theory of subjectivity in his study, *Gelegentlich Subjekt—Gestetz: Gestell: Gerüst* (Freiburg/Munich: Alber, 1983).

4. Dionysus Meets Diogenes; or, The Adventures of the Embodied Intellect

1. Sloterdijk's text here reads *"ein Denken auf der Suche nach dem verlorenen Orgiasmus"*; the title of the German translation of Proust's *À la recherche du temps perdu* is *Auf der Suche nach der verlorenen Zeit*. This would translate into English as "The Search for Lost Time," a more accurate equivalent of the French than *Remembrance of Things Past.*—Trans.

2. We should not overlook the fact that, during the initial phase of Eurpean structural scholarship—with the Pythagoreans—a conscious awareness of the nece·sary intersection between abstraction and ecstasy, theory and celebration (*Festlichkeit*), and mathematics and enthusiasm was still dominant, an awareness that resounds in authentic Platonisms and in an erotics of knowledge.

3. Nietzsche recounts the matter as follows: "The severest criticism that can be leveled against Socrates was made by a dream image. As he told his friends in prison, Socrates was visited repeatedly by the same dream, which always relayed the same message: 'Socrates, make music!' But to his last days Socrates had contented himself with the opinion that philosophy was the highest form of music. Finally he realized while in prison, in order to unburden his conscience, that he had to make a 'common' music as well. He actually set several prosaic fables that he knew to music, but I still do not believe he reconciled the muses with these metric exercises" (*Socrates und die Tragödie, KSA*, 1, p. 544).

4. Even as profound a student of Nietzsche as Giorgio Colli was disinclined to follow up on Nietzsche's "kynical" discovery. Colli was not prepared to understand the difference between cynicism as the infamy of the powerful and "kynicism" as the nobility (*noblesse*) of the powerless. For this reason he saw only the suspect satisfaction of the cynic at the collapse of the great men of whom he believed a priori that they were good for nothing. Colli correctly observed that "this was not Nietzsche's nature." He then incorrectly added the following: "It is therefore surprising to hear of him in *Ecce Homo* that he has here and there attained in his books the highest thing that can be achieved on earth—cynicism [*Zynismus*]" (*Nach Nietzsche* [Frankfurt: Athenäum, 1983], p. 70). Here we can see the result of a minor inattention on the part of the translator—Nietzsche always wrote "*Cynismus*"—along with the indifference of the Italian language to the distinction between "kynicism" and cynicism. Colli's surprise would be quickly dispelled if he were to place Nietzsche's literalization of philosophy into the proper context with the "cynical" form of speaking the truth. The editor should not forget Nietzsche's statement that "great subjects demand that one either keep silent about them or speak of them in great terms; by great I mean with innocence—cynically [*cynisch*]" (*KSA*, 13, p. 535).

5. See *Syllogismen der Bitterkeit* (Frankfurt: Suhrkamp, 1969), p. 32.

6. See Nietzsche's posthumous aphorism in the sketch, *From the War Academy of Life:* "Those who are deeply wounded possess an Olympic laughter; one has only what one needs" (*KSA*, 13, p. 531). More pointedly: "At that time I learned to *give* myself to art cheerfully, objectively, with curiosity, above all with health and mischievousness—and for a sick person, it seems to me, this is his

'good taste'? A more perceptive and sympathetic eye will not miss what perhaps constitutes the appeal of these writings—that a suffering and lacking person is speaking as if he were *not* suffering and lacking" (*KSA*, 2, p. 374).

7. See note 1, Chapter 3.

8. *PN,* p. 229.

9. *PN,* p. 332.

10. Nietzsche, *The Gay Science,* translated and with commentary by Walter Kaufmann (New York: Random House, 1974), p. 280.

11. Jacques Derrida comments at one point that "Nietzsche is the thinker of pregnancy" (*Spurs: Nietzsche's Style,* trans. Barbara Harlow [Chicago: University of Chicago Press, 1979], p. 65). I believe Nietzsche is something other than this, but something that is related to this idea nonetheless: the thinker of incarnation. Or, to be more precise, of the *subversion* of incarnation. Nietzsche's immoralism, in my opinion, is based not so much on a derestraining of the subject, because Nietzsche at no point underestimates the positive function of restraint as a means for providing intensification. To think incarnation means to expose violation (*Vergewaltigung*). The subversion of incarnation, therefore, refers not to a fascism of lack of restraint but, on the contrary, to a liberating game with the violent past. Nietzsche's "pregnancies" would thus be attempts to give life out of violation. The philosopher as a Kleistian Marquise of O? But this would also mean giving birth to centaurs.

12. Nietzsche very astutely made the point that the Dionysian vision, which is comparable to unlimited pain, becomes unbearable: "Five, six seconds and no more: then you suddenly feel the presence of eternal harmony. Man can, within his mortal frame, not endure it: he must either physically transform himself or die. It is a clear and indisputable feeling . . . if it were to last longer, the soul could not endure it; it would have to dissolve. In these five seconds I would live the whole of human existence, I would give my whole life for it, the price would not be too great. In order to endure it any longer, one would have to transform oneself physically" (*KSA*, 13, p. 145).

13. *PN,* p. 189.

14. A reference to the onset of Nietzsche's madness. In January of 1889, Nietzsche saw a coachman flogging a horse on the street in Turin. He threw his arms around the neck of the animal, collapsed, and remained insane until his death on August 25, 1900.—Trans.

15. Nietzsche wrote the following to Brandes on November 20, 1888, pertaining to his biography: "I have now narrated myself with a cynicism which will become world historical [*welthistorisch*]. The book is called *Ecce Homo* and is an attempted assassination without the least respect for the crucified one: it ends with thunder and lightning against everything that is Christian or infected with Christianity" (*KSA*, 15, p. 185).

16. See Nietzsche's letter to Jacob Burckhardt after he had gone mad, which begins with the words, "In the end I would much rather be a Basel professor than God" (*PN,* p. 685).

17. Cf. the following verse from "On the Poverty of the Richest One" from the last Dionysus dithyramb:

> Woe to you, Zarathustra!
> You look like someone
> Who has swallowed gold:
> Someone will slit your belly open!
>
> . . . .
> Be clever, you rich man!
> *Make a present of it to yourself first, O Zarathustra!*

5. Pain and Justice

1. The *Grundgesetz* is the provisory constitution of the Federal Republic of Germany.—Trans.

2. This thesis is, of course, overdrawn: one could speak here of the many voices of romantic protest that had already referred early on to a precarious affiliation between outer exoneration and an inner brutalization. The labor movement also represents a protest against the shifting of the burden from the old rural *misere* to modern proletarian misery.

3. For a definition of this term, see my *Critique of Cynical Reason*, trans. Michael Eldred (Minneapolis: University of Minnesota Press, 1987), p. 460: "Algodicy means a metaphysical interpretation of pain that gives it meaning. In modernity it takes the place of theodicy, as its converse. In the latter, it was asked, How are evil, pain, suffering and injustice to be reconciled with the existence of God? If there is no God and no higher meaning, how can we still bear the pain? The function of politics as a substitute theology immediately becomes clear."

4. From this point it is only one step further to a critique of cynical reason, i.e., to a reflection that elaborates on the concept of cynicism as the central category for the contemplation of culture and universal values in the post-Nietzschean situation.

5. Giorgio Colli, in his aphoristic meditations on the situation of the Western intellect "after Nietzsche," has brilliantly formulated this breakthrough by means of modern objectivist subjectivism. In a comment under the heading "The Other Dionysus," he says: "The symbol of the mirror, which attributes the Orphic tradition to Dionysus, lends the deity a metaphysical significance Nietzsche was not able to penetrate. Whenever the deity observes himself in the mirror, he sees the world as his own image. The world is thus a vision, and its nature is merely perception. The relationship between Dionysus and the world is that between the unspeakable godly life and its reflection. This does not offer the reflection of his face, but rather an unending multitude of creatures and celestial bodies, a monstrous stream of forms and colors—all of this is reduced to a reflection, to an image in the mirror. God does not create the world; the world is the god himself as phenomenon. That which we consider 'life,' the world around us, is the form in which Dionysus observes himself, expresses himself to himself. The Orphic symbol pushes the Western dichotomy between immanence and transcendence, a subject on which philosophers have wasted a lot of ink, into the realm of the ridiculous. There are not two things, about which one has to find out whether they are separate or unified; rather, there is only one thing, the god, and we are his hallucinations. Nietzsche approaches this version in *The Birth of Tragedy*, even if he does so with an excess of Schopenhauerian coloration; later a stubborn determination dims the immanence of his perspicacity" (*Nach Nietzsche* [Frankfurt: Athenäum, 1983], pp. 208-9). But does this dimming really occur? One would have to take into consideration this aphorism from *Beyond Good and Evil*: "Around the hero everything turns into a tragedy; around the demigod, into a satyr play; and around God—what? Perhaps into "world'?" (trans. Kaufmann [New York: Vintage, 1966], p. 150). I am not sure whether Nietzsche intended to reproach immanence with a stubborn determination. It seems to me that his anti-Platonic demeanor and his declaration of war against the beyond can be understood differently—as a martial accompaniment to the "great operation": the introversion of metaphysics. See also Chapter 4 of this essay.

6. See Martin Heidegger's *Nietzsche* (Pfullingen: Neske, 1961), vol. 1, pp. 639ff.

7. The twilight of the idols of the monarchy during the French Revolution was not alone in marking the first appearance of the postmetaphysical situation; neither was this situation marked only by the development of abstract atheism or of native sensualism and materialism in the British and French thought of the eighteenth century. The considerably more significant date in the history of a postmetaphysical thought and of Dionysian materialism—which must always at the same time be a dramatic, hermetic, and physiognomic materialism—is the birth of modern depth pyschology as mesmerism, animal magnetism, artificial somnambulism, and hypnotism around 1780. The piquant coexistence of these deepenings of subjectivity with a social occultism that is early socialist in nature has not yet been properly evaluated by intellectual historians. See Peter Sloterdijk, *Der Zauberbaum: Die Entstehung der Psychoanalyse im Jahr 1785* (Frankfurt: Suhrkamp, 1985).

8. I do believe in any case that we live in an era of overpoliticization, so that a certain depoliticizing of society in the course of the search for a *minimum of the political* could be counted as a plus.

I have borrowed the term ''antipolitical'' from the Hungarian writer György Konrád, who understood it to mean something along the line of spaces that were free of the influence of the state, and the moral and cultural wilfulness of society. See *Antipolitics: An Essay,* trans. Richard E. Allen (San Francisco: Harcourt Brace Jovanovich, 1984). I have suggested what antipolitics could signify under Western European conditions in my speech ''Taugenichts kehrt heim oder das Ende eines Alibis—Auch eine Theorie vom Ende der Kunst'' in my *Ende der Kunst—Zukunft der Kunst* (Munich, 1985), pp. 108–36.

Index

Index

Compiled by Hassan Melehy

Theory and History of Literature

Peter Sloterdijk holds a doctorate in German literature from the University of Hamburg with a concentration in the autobiographical literature of the Weimar Republic. Minnesota published his *Critique of Cynical Reason* in translation in 1988. His other books, published in German in the 1980s, include *Der Zauberbaum. Die Entstehung der Psychoanalysse im Jahr 1785 (an essay-novel on the origins of psychoanalysis), Kopernikanische Mobilmachung und ptolemäische Abrüstung* (on postmodern aesthetics), *Zur Welt kommen, Zur Sprache kommen. Frankfurter Poetik-Vorlesungen* (on poetics and maieutics, or the Socratic method), and *Eurotaoismus. Zur Kritik der politischen Kinetik* (a philosophy of posthistory).

Jamie Owen Daniel is currently working on a doctorate in the Modern Studies Program at the University of Wisconsin-Milwaukee. Her translations have appeared in *Telos*, *New German Critique*, and *October*.

Jochen Schulte-Sasse is director of graduate studies in the department of comparative literature and professor of German at the University of Minnesota. He is co-editor, with Wlad Godzich, of the series Theory and History of Literature.